Knit-a-bear

Knit-a-bear

15 fluffy friends to make and dress for every occasion

VAL PIERCE

First published 2014 by
Guild of Master Craftsman Publications Ltd
Castle Place, 166 High Street, Lewes,
East Sussex BN7 1XU

Text © Val Pierce, 2014
Copyright in the Work © GMC Publications
Ltd, 2014

ISBN 978 1 86108 977 9

Publisher Jonathan Bailey
Production Manager Jim Bulley
Managing Editor Gerrie Purcell
Senior Project Editor Dominique Page
Editor Jane Roe
Pattern Checker Jude Roust
Managing Art Editor Gilda Pacitti
Designer Ginny Zeal
Photographer Andrew Perris

Set in Geometric Slabserif and Doctor Soos
Colour origination by GMC Reprographics
Printed and bound in China

Contents

Introduction

Knitting a toy for a special person, whether they're young or old, can bring so much pleasure. An all-time favourite soft toy is the teddy bear. Most of us have had a treasured teddy at some point during our lives. Teddy bears appeal to all ages with their endearing expressions and soft, cuddly exteriors. They prove to be trusty playmates and friends, and children just love them.

In this book I have designed 15 bears, all of which have their own special characteristics. There's a ballet bear that will delight children who love to dance, an adventurous camouflage bear that is ready for action, a bedtime bear in pyjamas to snuggle up with at night and even a mother bear with her cub. Some have complete outfits with accessories; others are wearing just a simple top or waistcoat. Most of the bears are similar in size, so it is possible for you to change the clothes around and dress them in a new outfit each day.

Val

Before you start

Yarns

The array of yarns available can be overwhelming. Going into a yarn store is like entering Aladdin's cave with marvellous colours, textures and fibres everywhere you look. When choosing yarn to make toys it is wise to take into account the age of the person you will be knitting for. Babies and young children invariably put everything in their mouths, so using an eyelash yarn that may shed fibres isn't a good plan.

In this book, most of the yarns used are a good quality wool or wool mixture, because they work up nicely and give good stitch definition. They also wash well if needed. Some of the bears have been created using speciality type yarns that have a fluffy and furry appearance when worked up. I have stated a yarn weight for these yarns so it is possible to substitute them; however, do keep in mind that if you do, your finished project will not be identical to the one seen in this book.

Tension swatches

Each project has a suggested tension for the yarns used, and these are listed along with the materials section for each pattern. These are a guideline to help you when choosing your yarns. Tension is important for most knitting projects, but for toys it's a little different – if there is a slight discrepancy it won't cause too many problems. Obviously, if you do substitute yarns then your finished bear isn't going to look quite the same as the one in the book but it will still be a very lovable and unique character. See page 28 for more information about checking tension.

Speciality yarns

Some of the bears in the book have been made using speciality yarns. These give a more realistic appearance to the finished bear since they resemble fur. When stitching up with this yarn, use a large-eyed, blunt-ended needle and take care pulling the yarn through the work as you sew. It may not be possible for you to obtain the exact yarns I have used, but you will no doubt be able to substitute other similar yarns for them.

Yarn weights

Terminology for yarn weights varies from country to country. Below is a handy guide to common terms.

US	UK	Australia /NZ
Lace	2 ply	2 ply
Sock or Fingering	3 ply	3 ply
Fingering	4 ply	4 ply
Sport	Some double knitting yarns	5 ply
Light worsted	Double knitting	8 ply
Worsted	Aran	10 ply
Chunky	Bulky	16 ply
Bulky	Chunky	20 ply

Tools

As with all good recipes, the ingredients go a very long way to the success of the finished product. Substitute the word 'tools' for ingredients and the same principle applies to knitting. Having found a gorgeous pattern that you want to knit, it's no good embarking on your project without all the necessary basic equipment and knowledge needed to make it.

Knitting needles

There are many types of knitting needle available, ranging from metal, plastic and bamboo to beautiful rosewood needles. If you are just starting out then I suggest you choose some mid-range priced needles. Some come in sets, which is very useful since it is handy to have a variety of sizes. For the patterns in this book, you'll need sizes ranging from 3.25mm to 5.5mm (UK10:US3 to UK5:US9).

Needle size conversion chart

Different sizing systems are used around the world. The metric system is most commonly used in the UK, but it's useful to know the conversions.

Metric	UK	US
2mm	14	0
2.25mm	13	1
2.75mm	12	2
3mm	11	–
3.25mm	10	3
3.5mm	–	4
3.75mm	9	5
4mm	8	6
4.5mm	7	7
5mm	6	8
5.5mm	5	9
6mm	4	10
6.5mm	3	10.5
7mm	2	10.5
7.5mm	1	11
8mm	0	13
10mm	000	15

Other useful tools

A stitch holder is recommended, as it enables you to keep your stitches safe while you continue to knit.

Stitch counters are invaluable if you need to remember how many rows you have worked and are especially useful when working with some of the speciality yarns used in the book.

Stitch markers are used for marking a particular point in your work, such as a crucial bit of shaping. You can buy stitch markers or just tie a piece of yarn in a contrasting colour to the work.

It is also a good plan to have a couple of crochet hooks to hand in case you drop a stitch and need to work it up through the fabric.

A tape measure is an absolute must for checking the size of your work, as is a set of blunt-ended sewing needles with larger eyes to enable you to thread yarn easily through them when making up a garment or toy.

Last but by no means least, it is a great idea to have a knitting bag to keep all your projects safely stored away while you are not working on them.

Knitting techniques

Although most of the patterns in this book are quite straightforward, it is best if you have some knowledge of knitting before you start. To aid the novice knitter, in this chapter you will find a basic guide to all the stitches used in this book. The instructions given are for right-handed knitters, so if you are left-handed, you will need to reverse the hand-holding instructions.

Slip knot

The first thing you need to do is make a slip knot, which forms the first stitch.

1 Leave a tail of about 2in (5cm) and hold it in your left hand; hold the ball end of the yarn in your right hand. Wind the yarn around the forefinger on your left hand. Slide the yarn off your finger and pull it through to form a loop. Transfer the loop to the needle.

2 Pull the yarn tail down to tighten it.

Tip Numerous tutorials for practically every technique used in knitting can be found on the Internet. These give extra information and visual instructions if you feel unsure of what you are doing.

Casting on

Once you have made the slip knot, you can begin to cast on. Casting on will form the first row of stitches on your needle and one edge of the finished project, usually the bottom or hem edge. There are many ways to cast on but the following two methods are the most widely used.

The two-needle method

1 Make a slip knot about 4in (10cm) from the yarn end on one needle and hold this needle in your left hand. Insert the right-hand needle through the front loop and under the left-hand needle. Now pass the working yarn (i.e. the yarn attached to the ball) under and over the tip of the right-hand needle.

2 With your right-hand needle, draw the yarn through the slip knot to form a stitch.

3 Transfer the new stitch to your left-hand needle, placing it next to the slip knot. Continue in this way until you have the required number of stitches.

The one-needle or thumb method

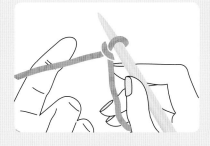 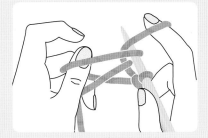 

1 Allow sufficient length of yarn from the main ball to enable you to cast on the required number of stitches (you'll need roughly 1in/2.5cm for each stitch). Make a slip knot on one needle and hold this in your right hand. Wind the tail-end of the yarn a round the thumb of your left hand, from front to back, and hold firm.

2 Insert the tip of the needle through the thumb loop from the front to the back and wind the yarn in your left hand around the back of the tip of the needle and between the needle and your thumb.

3 Pull the new loop through the thumb loop, thus forming a stitch. Slip the stitch onto the needle close to the slip knot. Continue in this way until you have the required amount of stitches.

Knit stitch

Now you have mastered casting on you can begin to form the first of two fundamental movements in knitting. The knit stitch forms a flat vertical loop on the fabric face. When working back and forth with only the knit stitch, you create a simple furrowed fabric known as garter stitch.

1 Hold the needle with the cast-on stitches in your left hand. Keeping the yarn behind the work, hold the second needle in your right hand and insert it into the front of the first stitch. With your right forefinger, take the yarn forward and around the right-hand needle.

2 Pull the yarn through to create a new loop.

3 Slide this new loop on to the right-hand needle. Continue for each stitch on the left-hand needle.

Purl stitch

The purl stitch is the other key stitch that is used in knitting. When used for every other row along with the knit stitch, it forms stocking stitch, which is flat and smooth on one side and more raised on the other. Once learned and mastered, these two stitches form the basis for a huge range of stitch patterns.

Working this method, the needle is put into the front of the stitch, then the yarn, which is held in the front, is wrapped over the back of the needle. Purl stitches tend to be a bit looser than knit ones so keep your fingers close to the work to help make the stitches more even.

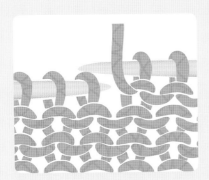

1 Hold the needle with the stitches on in your left hand. Keep the yarn at the front of the work.

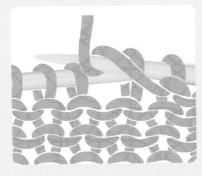

2 Insert the point of the right-hand needle into the front of the first stitch on the left-hand needle. With your right forefinger, take the yarn over the point of the right needle in an anti-clockwise direction.

3 Bring the needle back through the stitch and pull through, creating a new stitch. Drop the stitch onto the right-hand needle. Continue for each stitch on the left-hand needle.

Stitch patterns

Garter stitch
Cast on any number of stitches.
Knit every row.

Stocking stitch
Cast on any number of stitches.
Row 1 (right side): Knit.
Row 2 (wrong side): Purl.

Reverse stocking stitch
Cast on any number of stitches.
Row 1 (right side): Purl.
Row 2 (wrong side): Knit.

Moss stitch
Cast on an odd number of stitches.
Row 1: K1, *p1, k1; rep from * to
end. Repeat row 1.
This can also be worked as double
seed stitch on a multiple of four
stitches.
Rows 1 and 2: * K2, *p2; rep from
* to end of row.
Rows 3 and 4: *P2, *k2; rep from *
to end of row.

Rib stitch
K1, P1 or 1 x 1 ribbing: Single knit
stitches alternate with single purl
stitches, creating very narrow
columns. This stitch usually forms
the welts or neckbands on
garments and pulls in the work
quite tightly. To create K1, P1
ribbing, cast on an even number
of stitches.
Row 1: *K1, p1; rep from * to end
of row.
Repeat Row 1 for the length of
your piece.

Double rib stitch
K2, P2 or 2 x 2 ribbing: Alternates
two knit stitches with two purl
stitches. This stitch can also be
used for welts and neckbands but
it is more stretchy and pulls in less.
To create K2, P2 ribbing, cast on
a multiple of four stitches.
Row 1: *K2, p2; rep from * to end
of row
Repeat Row 1 for the length of
your piece.

Casting off

This technique is used to provide a finished edge at the end of your work. It is also used when shaping is needed and for making buttonholes. You would normally cast off in knit stitch on the right side of the work, but patterns will tell you if you need to cast off on the wrong side or using a different stitch. When casting off, be careful not to pull the stitches too tightly as this will result in a puckered edge and could make it difficult to sew up the garment.

1 Knit the first two stitches. Keeping the yarn at the back of the work, insert the needle through the first stitch on the right-hand needle. Lift the first stitch over the second stitch and let it drop off your needle.

2 Knit the next stitch so that you have two stitches on the right-hand needle again. Repeat the process until the desired number of stitches are cast off. You will have a single stitch left at the end of your casting off. Slip this off the needle, cut the yarn, run the end of yarn through the stitch and pull tightly to secure.

Practise

Now you have learned how to cast on, how to knit and purl and how to cast off. It's a good idea to practise all these techniques before moving on to the next section.

Increasing

When you are knitting a project that requires shaping you will need to add stitches, which is called increasing. This technique is also necessary when you are creating certain stitch patterns, such as lace.

Tip It is very important that you follow the particular method of increasing stated in the pattern you are following. As a rule the make one (M1 or m1) method is always mentioned in abbreviations for that pattern.

The bar method (kfb)

This frequently used method produces a small horizontal stitch on the right side of the work. You knit into the front and back of a stitch to make two stitches.

It creates a tiny 'bump' on the right side of the work so the increase is visible in the fabric but is not noticeable when worked on the edge of a garment.

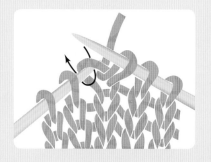

1 Knit a stitch in the usual way but do not remove it from the left-hand needle.

2 Insert the right-hand needle into the back of the same stitch and knit again. Move the stitch from the left-hand to the right-hand needle.

Make one (M1 or m1)

With this method you pick up the horizontal strand between two stitches and knit or purl into it to form a new stitch.

Insert your left-hand needle from front to back under the horizontal strand between two stitches.

Knit or purl into the back of the strand on your left-hand needle.

Transfer the stitch onto your right-hand needle. The twist in the stitch prevents a gap from appearing in the work.

Decreasing

Sometimes when you are knitting you have to lose several stitches in a row, such as when you are shaping a piece of a toy or working an armhole or neckline in a garment. Casting off is the normal method used when more than three stitches need to be lost. However, if only one or two stitches have to be decreased, either of the methods described below and on the next page can be used.

When working decreases on garments, they are normally done in pairs that are symmetrical, as on V-neck shaping or raglan sleeve shaping. Right slants are made by knitting or purling two stitches together through the front of both loops; left slants are made by working through the back of both loops. Slip stitch decreases slant in only one direction, from right to left in the knit stitch and from left to right in the purl stitch.

Knitting two stitches together (k2tog)

Right slant (k2tog)

1 Insert the tip of the right-hand needle in the next two stitches on the left-hand needle through the front of both loops. Take the yarn around the needle and draw it through.

2 Transfer the new stitch to your right-hand needle.

Left slant (k2tog tbl)

Insert the tip of the right-hand needle in the next two stitches on the left-hand needle through the back of both loops. Take the yarn around the needle.

Draw the thread through and transfer the new stitch to your right-hand needle.

The slip-stitch decrease

This results in a slightly looser decrease than knitting two stitches together. When made on a knit row it slants from right to left and is abbreviated Sl1, k1, psso. A similar decrease can be made on a purl row, when it slants from left to right. It is abbreviated Sl1, p1, psso.

On a knit row

Slip one stitch from your left-hand needle onto the right-hand needle without knitting it, then knit the next stitch.

Insert your left-hand needle into the front of the slipped stitch on the right-hand needle and pull it over the knitted one, as you do when casting off (see page 19). The right-to-left slant made by this decrease in a knit row is used on the right side of the centre of the work.

On a purl row

Slip one stitch from your left-hand needle onto the right-hand needle without purling it, then purl the next stitch.

Insert your left-hand needle into the front of the slipped stitch on the right-hand needle and pull it over the knitted one. The left-to-right slant made by this decrease in a purl row is used on the left side of the centre of the work.

Picking up stitches

When making toys or garments there are sometimes neckbands, collars and possibly edgings where you will need to pick up stitches from the edge of the knitted fabric. These stitches need to be picked up evenly all around the edge to give a neat, uniform finish.

To pick up a stitch from an edge

1 Hold the working yarn behind the completed piece and insert your knitting needle through it, between the rows and between the last two stitches of each row, from front to back.

2 Take the yarn over the needle as if knitting and draw a loop of the yarn through to form a stitch. Continue until the correct number of stitches has been formed.

Changing colours

Using different colours to enhance your projects is another technique that will bring fun to your knitting. In some of the patterns in the book you will need to knit stripes or work a motif into the fabric, so this section will tell you how to join in new colours or work with more than one colour in a row.

Working from a chart

Colour patterns are often charted on graph paper. Each square represents a stitch and each horizontal line of squares is a row of stitches. Some charts are coloured in while others are black and white and have a key at the side with different symbols depicting different shades. Charts are read from bottom to top and usually from right to left. They are normally in stocking stitch and odd numbered rows will be knit and even numbered rows will be purl. Therefore the first stitch of a chart

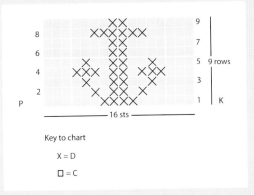

Key to chart

X = D

□ = C

is the bottom one on the right. Placing a straight edge, such as a ruler or bookmark, under each row will help you keep your place in the chart when working the design.

Adding new yarn at the start of a row

Use this method when working horizontal stripes.

Insert the right-hand needle into the first stitch on the left-hand needle and wrap the old and new yarns over the tip of the needle. Knit the stitch with both yarns.

Drop the old yarn and pick up the new yarn and continue to knit in the normal way.

Adding a new yarn within the row

Follow the method below when you will be using the original yarn again in the same row. The yarn not in use has to be carried along the back of the work; this is called stranding. This method is normally used over short distances, i.e. not more than four or five stitches. The weaving-in method is used when there are greater distances i.e. more than 6 stitches, and is done by twisting the yarn to be carried along the back of the work and around the yarn you are working with at the time. It forms a much denser fabric.

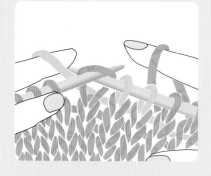

1 Leaving the old yarn at the back of your work, insert the right-hand needle into the stitch. Wrap the new yarn over the needle and use it for your new stitch.

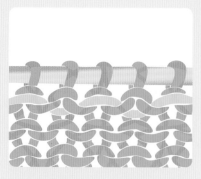

2 Continue knitting with the new yarn while carrying the old yarn across the back. On subsequent rows, purl the double stitches in the usual manner.

Intarsia

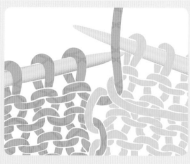

Intarsia is a technique used to incorporate areas of colour into your knitting. This could mean motifs or shapes. For each block of contrasting colour you will use a different length of yarn. The yarn is not carried across the back of the work, but rather twisted around the main colour at the edges of the secondary colour. It is useful to wind the smaller amounts of yarns needed onto bobbins to prevent tangled yarns while you work.

Swiss darning

This is a method of adding motifs to an already knitted garment, and, if done correctly, it looks as though the motif is actually knitted into the fabric. You will follow the chart as for the knitted version but instead of knitting the stitches you will work over each knitted stitch with the contrast yarn threaded into a blunt-ended needle. Each 'knit' stitch forms a V on the fabric and you will embroider the contrast yarn over this V to build up the motif.

Lace

Some of the patterns in this book use a lacy pattern so you will need to know how to create these stitches. These are abbreviated as either yo (yarn over) or yfwd (yarn forward), in either case they make a stitch and create a 'hole' in the fabric. You will then decrease a stitch in the same row to compensate and keep the stitch count the same.

Yarn over in stocking stitch (yo)

To make a yarn over in stocking stitch, bring the yarn forward to the front of the work as if you were going to make a purl stitch. Loop the yarn over your right-hand needle and knit the next stitch.

The loop and new stitch are now on your right-hand needle. Knit to the end of the row.

On the following row and with the rest of the stitches, purl the loop in the usual way.

Checking your tension

When knitting toys you do have to be careful with your tension, but not to the same extent as you would with a garment. A slight variation in size will not matter a great deal in a toy, but if you are going to substitute yarns then it is advisable to check the tension before starting on your project (see page 12 for the tension swatch information about yarns used in this book).

To check the tension, you need to make a tension swatch. This is a 4in (10cm) square made using the stitch pattern, yarn and needle size stated in the pattern.

Cast on the number of stitches and work the number of rows designated to give 4in (10cm). When you have completed your swatch, pin it to a flat surface. Do not stretch it.

Measure the swatch horizontally and vertically. If your tension does not match exactly that given in the pattern, change your needle size and knit another sample. One needle size will make a difference of about 1 stitch over 2in (5cm).

If your swatch is too small, your tension is too tight and you should change to a larger needle. If your swatch is too large, your tension is too loose and you should change to a smaller needle.

The type of yarn you use and the stitch pattern can also affect the tension, so it's important to make a sample if you are changing either one from that in the instructions.

When checking tension on a ribbed pattern, you need to pull the piece out to the correct width before measuring.

Tip Don't be afraid to change your needles. As long as the tension works out correctly your knitting is going to turn out the right size for that pattern.

Correcting mistakes

While you are knitting it's always a good idea to check your work regularly for any errors; the sooner you pick up on them the quicker you'll be able to put them right

Mark the row where the mistake occurred using a stitch marker at the end of the row. Carefully take your work off the needles and pull it back until you are one row above the error. To replace the stitches back onto the needle, hold the yarn at the back of the work, insert the left needle into the front row of the first stitch below the unpicked row. Pull on the working yarn to remove the top stitch.

If you drop a stitch and it unravels down the fabric, use a crochet hook to retrieve the stitch and work it up row by row picking up the strand of yarn behind the stitch on every row until you reach the top. Slip the stitch back onto the needle and continue working in the normal way.

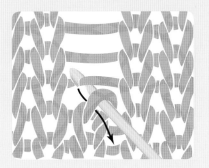

Making up

Having spent many hours knitting all the pieces to make your toy you now have to stitch all the pieces together and add the details. Don't be tempted to rush this step; clumsy seaming can ruin an otherwise beautifully knitted project.

Sewing together

Toys need to be sewn together securely since they may have to withstand many hours of playtime and be pulled around by little hands. Go over areas more than once when sewing on arms, legs and heads to ensure they won't pull off. Seams must also be sewn up securely – a backstitch seam works well for toys.

Very often toys' heads will appear to wobble when sewn in place and, seemingly, no matter how hard you try it is impossible to get them firm. This is a result of the head and body not being equally stuffed, i.e., if the head is too heavy then it will not sit correctly, and the same if the body is too solid and the head is under-stuffed. You can always add a little more stuffing to a piece by opening a tiny part of the seam, or you can remove stuffing in the same way.

To sew a head to a body catch it in place firstly with a few stitches placed around the neck edge. This will hold it steady while you then begin to sew the two pieces in place more firmly. Take a stitch from the body and one from the head all the way around, pulling the yarn firmly. Check all the time that the head is straight, not too far back or too far forward. Mostly toys' heads will all be facing front and straight. Sometimes to get a really cute look on animals it is possible to angle the head very slightly.

Some of the bears in the book have the head and body knitted all in one piece. The head is then formed by running a thread all around a specifically marked row at the neck edge. The head part is stuffed first and then a needle threaded with matching yarn is woven in and out of each stitch on the marked row, starting and ending at the centre back. The yarn is then pulled quite tightly, forming the head as you do so. You must make sure that the yarn is securely held when starting and finishing since if it should come undone then you will spoil the toy.

Joining seams

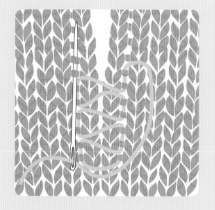

There are various ways of joining seams on knitted fabrics. Garter stitch can be sewn up with the right sides of the pieces facing you. Catch the 'tiny bumps' on the fabric together alternately from the pieces you are joining and pull them together quite firmly as you do. This will result in an almost invisible seam. You can join stocking stitch the same way by picking up the horizontal strand between the V stitches on alternate pieces on the fabric to be joined and pulling it quite tightly – this is termed mattress stitch.

Stuffing and adding features

Stuffing toys and adding features are sometimes daunting tasks for inexperienced workers. Refer to the picture of the toy you are making. Always use safety stuffing and use small amounts at a time, teasing out the stuffing as you fill the piece of knitting. This will eliminate large, lumpy looking bodies and heads and ensure a smooth and even feel to the toy. Don't over- or under-stuff your toy, and try to get arms and legs as even as possible, so check they match in size and circumference as you work.

Wobbly heads can often be a huge problem when making toys – this is often caused by either the head or body being over or under stuffed. Where there are clothes in a pattern

for a toy, these may not fit properly if the toy is over- or under-stuffed. I have provided dimensions for the waist measurements of the bears to help with this problem.

Adding the features is the final stage. Once again, look at the picture of the toy you are making and place markers for the eyes and nose. Look at the size of the eyes you need to add. Practise stitches on a spare piece of fabric and when you feel confident then work on your toy. If it doesn't look right, carefully unpick and try again. Patience is always rewarded where this is concerned.

Noses can be embroidered using straight stitches worked close together. Most of the noses in this

book are knitted, making it easier for you. When embroidering eyes, start with a French knot (see page 32) on one side, pull through to the other eye position and work a second French knot. Now continue to work extra stitches on each eye, pulling through alternately to either eye. This will also help to shape the nose. Don't pull in too tightly though or you will distort the face.

As with anything, practise makes perfect so don't be disheartened if you are not satisfied with your first attempts. Just keep on trying and you will achieve the results you want.

Twisted cord

Measure a length (or the number of lengths called for in the pattern) of yarn approximately four times longer than the desired length of finished cord. Fold the strand(s) in half and make a slipknot at the cut ends. Pass the slipknot over a doorknob or chair back spindle to anchor it and stand far enough away that the yarn comes straight out from the anchor, parallel to the floor.

Slip a crochet hook or pencil into the folded end and twist the yarn until it becomes taut.

Remove the end from the anchor, grasp the centre of the twisted yarn and bring the ends together. Release the ends and the cord will twist on itself. Knot the ends.

Tassel

Cut a piece of cardboard that is approximately twice the depth of your finished tassel. Wind the yarn around the card about fifteen or twenty times.

Thread matching yarn through the wraps at one end of the cardboard and tie around the top of the tassel tightly. Cut the yarn ends at the other end of the cardboard and remove.

Wrap a separate piece of yarn six times around the tassel about 1in (2.5cm) from the tied end. Fasten off and push the yarn end inside the tassel to keep it neat. Trim the loose ends to make them even. Attach to a twisted cord if desired.

SAFETY

Safety is paramount when finishing off toys, especially if they are intended for very young children. Do not use buttons or beads on toys that will be given to babies or toddlers. You will see that I have not used buttons on any of the clothes for the teddy bears.

If you intend to use safety eyes, make sure they are properly fixed into the fabric. They consist of a plastic eye with a grooved shank, and a washer that pushes onto the back of the shank. You will hear the washer click into place when it's secured.

Decorative embroidery

Simple embroidery stitches can add colour and texture to a knitted garment.
I have used very simple embroidery stitches, such as chain stitch and lazy daisy
stitch, to create flowers and leaves. These are best worked with blunt-ended
needles so that you don't split the fabric when working through it.

French knot

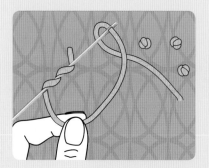

Bring the needle out of the knitted background from back to front; wrap the yarn around the needle two or three times. Use your thumb to hold it in place while pulling the needle through the wraps into background a short distance from where it came out. The more times you wrap the yarn around the needle, the bigger the 'knot'.

Chain stitch

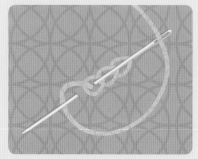

Start by bringing your needle up through the fabric as you would with any other stitch, then bring the needle back down through the same hole, slowly, in order to form a loop. Gently lay the loop flat against the fabric. Then, push the needle up on the inside of the tip of the loop. Push the needle back through the fabric again, this time securing the loop just made. The first chain is made. Continue in this manner to create consecutive loops.

Lazy daisy stitch

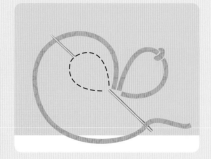

This stitch is formed in the same way as a chain stitch but each 'chain' is radiated from the same central point to form a flower or leaf shape.

Abbreviations & terminology

Abbreviations

alt	alternate
beg	beginning
cm	centimetre
dec	decrease
foll	following
in	inch
inc	increase
k	knit
kfb	knit front and back
m1	make 1
p	purl
patt	pattern
psso	pass slipped stitch over
RS	right side
rem	remaining
rep	repeat
skpo	sl1, k1, pass slipped stitch over
st	stitch
st st	stocking stitch
tbl	through back of loop
tog	together
WS	wrong side
yfwd	yarn forward over needle to make a hole
yrn	yarn round needle

UK and US terminology

UK	US
Cast off	Bind off
Moss stitch	Seed stitch
Stocking stitch	Stockinette stitch
Yarn forward	Yarn over

The Projects

Henry

With his striped sweater, jolly neckerchief and jaunty sailor's cap, Henry is sure to become a favourite companion for girls and boys alike. An anchor is knitted into the front of his sweater, but it can be Swiss-darned onto the fabric instead if you prefer.

YOU WILL NEED

For Henry

Rico Fashion Fur, 85% acrylic, 15% nylon (87yds/80m per 50g ball):
2 x 50g balls in 002 Grey (A)
Sirdar Snuggly DK, 55% nylon, 45% acrylic (179 yds/165m per 50g ball):
1 x 50g ball in 436 Light Grey (B)
Oddment of dark grey yarn for features

Needles size 5.5mm (UK5:US9)
Needles size 4mm (UK8:US6)
Safety stuffing

For the sailor outfit

Sirdar Snuggly DK, 55% nylon, 45% acrylic (179yds/165m per 50g ball):
1 x 50g ball white (C)
1 x 50g ball red (D)
1 x 50g ball navy (E)

Needles size 4mm (UK8:US6)

KNITTING NOTES

Tension

12 sts x 16 rows to 4in (10cm) for Fashion Fur using 5.5mm (UK5:US9) needles.
22 sts and 28 rows to 4in (10cm) for DK yarn using 4mm (UK8:US6) needles.

Yarn notes

You may substitute the yarns listed for any eyelash or double knitting weight yarns, but do check your tension. By substituting the yarns your bear will not look quite the same as the one in the book.

Measurements

11in (28cm) tall when sitting. Circumference of tummy when stuffed is about 13½in (34.5cm).

Abbreviations

Refer to page 33.

Tip It isn't easy to count rows in this type of yarn so take care to mark down the rows as you work.

Henry

Head

Using 5.5mm needles and A, cast on 10 sts.

Next row: Purl.

Next row: Inc in each stitch across row (20 sts).

Beg with a purl row, work 3 rows st st.

Next row: *K1, inc in next st; rep from * to end (30 sts).

Beg with a purl row, work 3 rows st st.

Next row: *K1, inc in next st; rep from * to end (45 sts).

Beg with a purl row, work 11 rows st st.

Shape top of head

Next row: *K1, k2tog; rep from * to end of row (30 sts).

Beg with a purl row, work 3 rows st st.

Next row: K2tog across row (15 sts).

Next row: Purl.

Break yarn and run through sts left on needle. Draw up and fasten off.

Body

Using 5.5mm needles and A, cast on 10 sts.

Next row: Purl.

Next row: Inc in each stitch across row (20 sts).

Beg with a purl row, work 3 rows st st.

Next row: *K1, inc in next st; rep from * to end (30 sts).

Beg with a purl row, work 3 rows st st.

Next row: *K1, inc in next st; rep from * to end (45 sts).

Beg with a purl row, cont in st st. Work a further 35 rows.

Shape top of body

Next row: *K1, k2tog; rep from * to end of row (30 sts).

Beg with a purl row, work 3 rows st st.

Next row: K2tog all across row (15 sts).

Next row: Purl.

Break yarn and run through sts left on needle. Draw up and fasten off.

Muzzle

Using 4mm needles and B, cast on
8 sts.

Next row: Purl.

Next row: Inc in each st across
row (16 sts).

Next row: Purl.

Next row: *K1, inc in next st; rep
from * to last st, k1 (24 sts).

Next row: Purl.

Work 4 rows st st.

Next row: *K1, inc in next st; rep
from * to end (36 sts).

Work in st st for 6 rows and cast off.

Legs
make 2

Using 5.5mm needles and A, cast
on 8 sts.

Next row: Purl.

Next row: Inc in each st across
row (16 sts).

Work in st st for 5 rows.

Next row: Inc 1 st at each end of
row (18 sts).

Work 3 rows st st.

Next row: *K2, inc in next st; rep
from * to end (24 sts).

Work 11 rows st st.

Next row: *K1, k2tog; rep from * to
end (16 sts).

Work 7 rows st st.

Next row: K5, inc in each of next
6 sts, k5 (22 sts).

Next row: Purl.

Next row: K5, (k1, inc1) 6 times, k5
(28 sts).

Work 5 rows st st and cast off
fairly loosely.

Arm pads
make 2

Using 4mm needles and B, cast on
8 sts.

Next row: Purl.

Next row: K1, inc1, knit to last
2 sts, inc1, k1 (10 sts).

Next row: Purl.

Cont to inc as on last 2 rows to
14 sts.

Work in st st for 9 rows. Cast off.

Arms
make 2

Using 5.5mm needles and A, cast
on 8 sts.

Next row: Purl.

Next row: Inc in each st across
row (16 sts).

Next row: Purl.

Work 4 rows st st.

Next row: Inc 1 st at each end
(18 sts).

Work 13 rows st st.

Next row: *K2, inc in next st; rep
from * to end (24 sts).

Work 7 rows st st.

Next row: K2tog across row
(12 sts).

Next row: Purl.

Next row: K2tog across row (6 sts).

Cast off.

Feet pads
make 2

Using 4mm needles and B, cast on
8 sts.

Next row: Purl.

Now inc 1 st at each end of next
and following alt rows until you
have 14 sts.

Knit 11 rows in st st.

Dec 1 st at each end of next and
following alt rows until you have
8 sts. Cast off.

Ears
make 2

Using 5.5mm needles and A, cast
on 8 sts.

Next row: Purl.

Next row: Inc knitwise in each st
across row (16 sts).

Work 5 rows st st.

Next row: K2tog across row (8 sts).

Next row: Purl.

Next row: K2tog across row (4 sts).
Cast off.

To make up

Sewing up with this type of yarn needs care. Use a big-eyed, blunt-ended needle and short lengths of yarn. Seams will run down the back of the head and body, and the undersides of the arms and legs.

Sew the body seam first, leaving the cast-on end open to stuff. Stuff firmly to give a nice rounded shape. Close the gap. Sew the head in the same way, leaving an opening to stuff. Stuff firmly. Sew the seams on the arms and, as before, leave an edge open to enable stuffing. To stuff the arms, push plenty of stuffing down into the paw first then continue stuffing the rest of the arm. Pin the arm pads in position on each lower paw. Sew neatly in place.

Sew the seams on the legs, leaving the base open to enable you to sew on the foot pads. Pin each foot pad in place all around the foot opening; add more stuffing if needed. Carefully sew the foot pad in place all around the opening. With dark grey yarn, embroider claws on the paws and feet with long stitches.

Take the muzzle and sew the seam, this will run underneath. Pin to the front of the bear's head and add stuffing to give shape. This will take a bit of time and patience to get it to look good. Now sew the muzzle onto the face, adding more stuffing to give a good shape. Embroider a nose and mouth with black yarn, and then eyes. Pin the ears onto either side of the head. Try to get them level. Take some matching yarn, curl the ears into a semi-circular shape, then stitch in place onto the head.

Now assemble the bear, noting he is in the sitting position. Pin the legs in place first, getting them level if you can. Sew in place. Pin the arms in position as you did with the legs. Sew firmly in place. Finally, sew the bear's head onto the body.

Sailor outfit

Sweater back

Using 4mm needles and E, cast on 42 sts.

Work 6 rows in k2, p2 rib.

Change to st st and join in C (carry yarn not in use neatly up the side of the work).

Proceed as follows:

Rows 1–4: Using C, work 4 rows in st st.

Rows 5–6: Pick up E and work 2 rows garter st.

Rep the last 6 rows 4 times more, then work rows 1–4 again. Break C and join in E.

Next row: Knit.

Next row: Work in k2, p2 rib. Work 3 more rows in rib and cast off.

Sweater front

You will use separate balls of red and navy yarns while working the anchor and stripe pattern.

Using 4mm needles and E, cast on 42 sts.

Work 6 rows in k2, p2 rib.

Change to st st and join in C (carry yarn not in use neatly up the side of the work).

Proceed as follows:

Rows 1–4: Using C, work 4 rows in st st.

Rows 5–6: Pick up E and work 2 rows garter st.

Rep rows 1–6 once more.

Then work rows 1–4 again.

Now proceed to work anchor motif as follows and at the same time

keeping continuity of the 6-row stripe pattern:

Row 1: K14 E, work row 1 of chart over next 16 sts, k14 E.

Cont to work from chart until row 9 is completed. Break D.

Now work in stripe pattern as before over all sts and complete to match back.

Sleeves
make 2

Using 4mm needles and E, cast on 42 sts.

Work 6 rows in k2, p2 rib.

Change to st st and join in C (carry yarn not in use neatly up the side of the work).

Proceed as follows:

Rows 1–4: Using C, work 4 rows in st st.

Rows 5–6: Pick up E and work 2 rows garter st.

Rep rows 1–6 twice more then rows 1–4 again.

Cast off.

To make up

Overlap rib on shoulders from front to back for ¾in (2cm) on either side. Sew together to form boat-shape neck. Fold one sleeve in half and mark the centre point. Lay the sweater out flat and pin centre point of sleeve to shoulder join. Join sleeve to sweater on back and front, making sure each side is equal. Do the same with the other sleeve. Now join side and sleeve seams, matching the stripes.

ANCHOR CHART (16 sts x 9 rows)

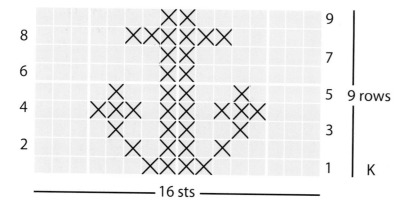

Key to chart

X = D

☐ = C

Cap

Using 4mm needles and E, cast on 54 sts.

Work 5 rows in garter st.

Change to st st and C.

Work 4 rows in st st.

Next row: K1, *k1, inc in next st; rep from * to last st, k1 (80 sts).

Next row: Purl.

Work 10 rows st st.

Decrease for the crown

Row 1: *K8, k2tog; rep from * to end (72 sts).

Row 2 and following alt rows: Purl.

Row 3: *K7, k2tog; rep from * to end (64 sts).

Row 5: *K6, k2tog; rep from * to end (56 sts).

Cont decreasing as set working 1 less stitch in each rep until you have reached the row * K1, K2tog, rep from * to end.

Next row: Purl.

Next row: K2tog all across row. Break yarn and run through sts on needle, draw up tight and secure.

Peak

Using 4mm needles and E, cast on 15 sts.

Work 6 rows in garter st.

Next row: K2tog at each end of the row (13 sts).

Repeat last row until you have 7 sts. Cast off.

To make up

Join side seam on cap, sew peak to centre front.

Neckerchief

Using 4mm needles and D, cast on 3 sts.

Row 1: Knit.

Row 2: Inc in first and last st (5 sts).

Row 3: Knit (5 sts).

Row 4: K2, p1, k2.

Row 5: K2, m1, k1, m1, k2 (7 sts).

Row 6: K2, p3, k2.

Row 7: K2, m1, k3, m1, k2 (9 sts).

Row 8: K2, p5, k2.

Cont to inc 1 st at each end of every other row until you have 38 sts. Work 4 rows without further increase maintaining the k2 borders on either side as before. Now divide for the neck ties as follows:

Next row: Knit.

Next row: K2, p6, knit to last 8 sts, p6, k2.

Next row: Knit.

Next row: K2, p4, k2, cast off centre 22 sts, k2, p4, k2.

Proceed on the first set of 8 sts for tie.

Next row: K8.

Next row: K2, p4, k2.

Repeat the last 2 rows 9 times more.

Next row: K2, skpo, k2tog, K2 (6 sts).

Next row: K2, p2, k2.

Next row: K6.

Next row: K2, p2, k2.

Next row: K2, k2tog, k2 (5 sts).

Next row: Knit.

Work 12 rows garter st on these sts.

Next row: K2tog, k1, k2tog (3 sts).

Next row: Knit.

Next row: K3tog and fasten off.

Return to remaining set of sts and complete to match first side.

To make up

Using white yarn, work 'spots' in a random pattern onto the neckerchief with French knots (see page 32).

Princess Gracie

Every toy box needs a princess, so why not make Gracie, a special teddy bear with her very own sparkly crown and dress? Knitted in a snuggly yarn that is so soft to touch, she will be a pleasure to cuddle.

YOU WILL NEED

For Princess Gracie

Bergère de France Plume, 47% polyamide, 42% acrylic, 11% wool (65yds/60m per 50g ball): 3 x 50g balls in 24793 Tulle (A)
Small amount of brown DK yarn (B)
Oddment of brown 4-ply for features

Needles size 5.5mm (UK5:US9)
Needles size 4mm (UK8:US6)
Safety stuffing

For the dress and crown

1 x 50g ball Wendy Peter Pan DK shade 928 (C)
1 x 50g ball Wendy Chic in shade pink and silver (D)
Small amount of Twilleys Gold Fingering Yarn shade Gold for crown (E)

Needles size 4mm (UK8:US6)
Needles size 3.25mm (UK10:US3)
Ribbon roses, ribbon bows
and narrow matching ribbon

KNITTING NOTES

Tension

24 sts x 32 rows to 4in (10cm) for Wendy Peter Pan DK using 4mm (UK8:US6) needles.
15 sts x 20 rows to 4in (10cm) for Bergère de France Plume using 5.5mm (UK5:US9) needles.

Yarn notes

This bear is worked entirely in garter stitch.

Measurements

12in (30cm) tall when sitting. Circumference of tummy when stuffed is about 14in (35.5cm).

Abbreviations

Refer to page 33.

Princess Gracie

Head

Using 5.5mm needles and A, cast on 42 sts.

Knit 4 rows.

Next row: K2tog at each end of row (40 sts).

Knit 2 rows.

Cont shaping as on last 3 rows until 4 sts remain.

Next row: K2tog twice (2 sts).

Next row: K2tog and fasten off.

Muzzle

Using 5.5mm needles and A, cast on 10 sts.

Inc 1 st at each end of next 2 rows.

Cast on 2 sts at beg of next 2 rows.

Knit 6 rows straight.

Cast off 2 sts at beg of next 2 rows.

K2tog at each end of next 3 rows.

Knit 2 rows and then cast off.

Body

make 2

Using 5.5mm needles and A, cast on 16 sts.

Knit 4 rows.

Inc 1 st at each end of next and following alt rows until you have 26 sts.

Knit 36 rows.

Dec 1 st at each end of next and following alt rows until 14 sts remain.

Cast off. (This is the neck edge.)

Arms

make 2

Using 5.5mm needles and A, cast on 8 sts.

Knit 1 row.

Next row: Inc in each stitch across row (16 sts).

Knit 2 rows.

Inc 1 st at each end of next and alt rows until you have 22 sts.

Knit 28 rows.

Decrease for top of arm

Next row: K2tog at each end of row.

Next row: Knit.

Repeat last 2 rows once more.

Cast off. (This is the top of the arm.)

Legs

make 2

Using 5.5mm needles and A, cast on 18 sts.

Knit 1 row.

Next row: Inc in each stitch across row (36 sts).

Knit 16 rows.

Next row: K14, k2tog 4 times, k14 (32 sts).

Next row: Knit.

Next row: K14, k2tog twice, k14 (30 sts).

Knit 26 rows.

Next row: K2tog at each end of row (28 sts).

Next row: Knit.

Next row: K2tog across row (14 sts).

Cast off.

Outer ears

make 2

Using 5.5mm needles and A, cast on 8 sts.

Knit 1 row.

Inc 1 st at each end of next 5 rows (18 sts).

Work 4 rows straight.

Next row: K2tog across row.

Cast off.

Inner ears
make 2
Work as outer ears but use B instead of A and 4mm needles.

To make up
Follow the diagrams on the right to show you how to sew the head together. Stuff the head and get a nice shape. Sew the ears together in pairs of one inner and one outer, then attach on either side of the head. Curl them slightly when stitching to give a pleasing shape. Take the muzzle and stitch it in place on the head, stuffing lightly to give a nice shape. Embroider eyes, nose and mouth with 4-ply brown yarn, using the photographs as a guide.

Sew the two body sections together, leaving the neck edge open for stuffing. Stuff firmly and shape, then close the opening. Sew up the arms. The seams should be at the centre back, leaving the top open for stuffing and shaping. After stuffing, close the gap. Sew the leg seams but leave the top of the leg open. Stuff and shape, then sew up the opening. Attach the arms and legs firmly to the body. The teddy is in a sitting position so attach the legs accordingly.

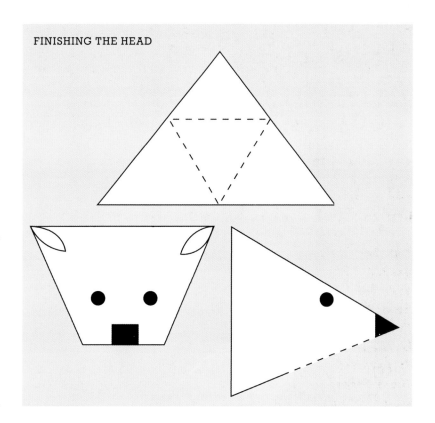

FINISHING THE HEAD

Dress & crown

Dress

make 2

Using 4mm needles and C, cast on 36 sts.

Work in st st for 8 rows.

Shape armholes

Cast off 3 sts at beg of next 2 rows (30 sts).

Next row: K2, skpo, knit to last 4 sts, k2tog, k2 (28 sts).

Next row: K2, purl to last 2 sts, k2.

Repeat last 2 rows twice more.

Next row: K2, skpo, knit to last 4 sts, k2tog, k2 (22 sts).

Knit 3 rows in garter stitch.

Divide for neck and straps

Next row: K5, cast off 12 sts, k5.

Cont on first set of 5 sts for straps. Work in garter stitch for 14 rows and cast off. Return to remaining 5 sts and work to match first strap.

Work skirt as follows

With right side facing and using 4mm needles and C, pick up and knit 36 sts from cast on edge.

Next row: Knit.

Next row (ribbon hole row): K1, *yfwd, k2tog; rep from * to last st, k1.

Next row: Knit.

Next row: Knit but increase in each st across row (72 sts).

Next row: Purl, but increase in first and last sts (74 sts).

Begin lacy pattern:

Row 1: K1, *(k2tog) 3 times, (yfwd, k1) 6 times, (k2tog) 3 times; rep from * to last st, k1.

Row 2: Knit.

Row 3: Change to D, knit.

Row 4: Using D, purl.

Row 5: Using C, repeat row 1.

Row 6: Knit.

Row 7: Knit.

Row 8: Purl.

These 8 rows form pattern. Repeat these 8 rows 3 more times. Work 4 rows in garter stitch using D. Cast off.

To make up

Join the side seams, taking care to match the pattern. Sew the shoulder strap seams. Thread a length of ribbon through the holes at the waist. Add ribbons and roses as in the photos. Slip the dress onto the bear and then tie the ribbon at the waist to gather up the skirt of the dress.

Crown

Points of crown (make 5) You will use two strands of yarn knitted together for these points.

Using 3.25mm needles and E, cast on 2 sts.

Next row: Knit.

Next row: Inc in first st, k1 (3 sts).

Next row: Knit.

Next row: Inc in first and last sts (5 sts).

Next row: Knit.

Cont to inc at each end of next and following alt row (9 sts).

Next row: Knit.

Slip sts onto stitch holder.

Make 4 more points in the same way, slipping each point onto the stitch holder.

Base of crown (Use single strand of yarn)

Using 3.25mm needles and E, knit across each point from stitch holder (45 sts).

Next row: Purl.

Next row: Knit.

Now work 4 rows in garter st and cast off.

To make up

Sew in the ends carefully. Join the short ends of the piece. Now thread a needle with some metallic yarn and sew the points together at the base to make the points stand up. Attach to the bear's head.

Big Ted

With his camouflage top and bandana to match, little adventurers are going to love this tough camo bear. He is all ready for an action-packed outing. Simple stitches are used to create him and his clothes, so a novice could easily attempt this design.

YOU WILL NEED

For Big Ted
Peter Pan DK, 55% nylon, 45% acrylic (195 yds/178m per 50g ball):
2 x 50g balls Deep Brown shade 915 (A)
1 x 50g ball Peter Pan Mid Brown shade 929 (B)
Oddments of black and white DK yarn for features

Needles size 4mm (UK8:US6)
Safety stuffing

For sweater and bandana
1 x 50g ball West Yorkshire Spinners Aire Valley Shade 814 (C)

Needles size 4mm (UK8:US6)

KNITTING NOTES

Tension
24 sts x 32 rows to 4in (10cm) using 4mm (UK8:US6) needles.

Yarn notes
Random-dyed camouflage yarn is used for the bandana and sweater, but dark green yarn would work just as well.

Measurements
12in (30cm) tall when sitting. Circumference of tummy when stuffed is about 13¾in (35cm).

Abbreviations
Refer to page 33.

Big Ted
Body and head
made all in one piece

Using 4mm needles and A, cast on 20 sts.

Next row: Purl.

Next row: Inc in each st across row (40 sts).

Next row: Purl.

Next row: *K1, inc in next st; rep from * to end (60 sts).

Cont in st st for 44 more rows.

Decrease row (mark this row for neck of bear)

Next row: *K4, skpo; rep from * to end (50 sts).

Next row: Purl.

Cont on these 50 sts for a further 26 rows.

Shape top of head

Next row: *K5, skpo; rep from * to last st, k1 (43 sts).

Next and following alt rows: Purl.

Next row: *K4, skpo; rep from * to last st, k1 (36 sts).

Next row: *K3, skpo; rep from * to last st, k1 (29 sts).

Next row: *K2, skpo; rep from * to last st, k1 (22 sts).

Next row: *K1, skpo; rep from * to last st, k1 (15 sts).

Next row: Skpo; rep to last st, k1 (8 sts).

Purl 1 row and cast off.

Muzzle

Using 4mm needles and B, cast on 10 sts.

Next row: Purl.

Next row: Inc in each st across row (20 sts).

Next row: Purl.

Next row: *K1, inc in next st; rep from * to end (30 sts).

Next row: Purl.

Next row: *K2, inc in next st; rep from * to end (40 sts).

Next row: Purl.

Next row: *K3, inc in next st; rep from * to end (50 sts).

Next row: Purl.

Next row: *K4, inc in next st; rep from * to end (60 sts).

Next row: Purl.

Work 4 rows in st st and cast off.

Ears
make 4
Using 4mm needles and B, cast on 10 sts.

Work in st st for 2 rows.

Next row: Inc in each st across row (20 sts).

Beg with a purl row, work 9 rows in st st.

Next row: K2tog across row (10 sts).

Next row: Purl.

Next row: K2tog across row and cast off.

Arms
make 2
Using 4mm needles and A, cast on 10 sts.

Next row: Purl.

Next row: *K1, inc in next st; rep from * across row (15 sts).

Next row: Purl.

Next row: *K1, inc in next st; rep from * to last st, k1 (22 sts).

Next row: Purl.

Next row: Inc in first and last st (24 sts).

Beg with a purl row, work 27 rows in st st.

Next row: *K1, skpo; rep from * to end (16 sts).

Next row: Purl.

Next row: K2tog across row (8 sts).

Next row: Purl.

Next row: K2tog across row (4 sts).

Break yarn and run through sts left on needle. Draw up and fasten off.

Legs
make 2
Using 4mm needles and A, cast on 10 sts.

Next row: Purl.

Next row: *K1, inc in next st; rep from * across row (15 sts).

Next row: Purl.

Next row: *K1, inc in next st; rep from * to last st, k1 (22 sts).

Next row: Purl.

Next row: Inc in first and last st (24 sts).

Next row: Purl.

Repeat last 2 rows once more (26 sts).

Cont in st st for 24 rows.

Increase for foot

Next row: K9, inc in each of next 8 sts, k9 (34 sts).

Next row: Purl.

Next row: K12, inc in each of next 10 sts, k12 (44 sts).

Beg with a purl row, work 9 rows st st.

Next row: K2tog across row (22 sts).

Next row: Purl.

Next row: K2tog across row (11 sts).

Next row: Purl.

Next row: K2tog across row to last st, k1 (6 sts).

Break yarn and run through sts left on needle. Draw up and fasten off.

Nose

Using 4mm needles and A, cast on
8 sts.

Work 4 rows in st st.

Next row: K2tog, work to last 2 sts,
k2tog (6 sts).

Next row: Purl.

Next row: K2tog, k2, k2tog (4 sts).

Next row: Purl.

Next row: K2tog twice (2 sts).

Next row: Purl.

Next row: K2tog and fasten off.

Leave a long tail of yarn as you will
use this to form the mouth.

To make up

Begin with the head and body
of the bear. Sew the seam that
runs down the back of the bear.
Leave the base open to stuff.

Stuff the head first, making it
firm and round. Thread a needle
with matching yarn and, beginning
at the marked row for the neck,
weave the yarn in and out of each
stitch all the way around, starting
and ending at the seam. Pull up
quite firmly to form the head and
neck. Secure well at the seam.
Continue to stuff the body, then
close the base.

Sew the side seam of the muzzle
to form a cup shape, add some
stuffing then pin it to the front of the
head. Use the photos as a guide.

Sew the muzzle in place. Pin the
nose in the centre of the muzzle,
with the widest part at the top.
Add a tiny bit of stuffing to pad it
out slightly, then sew in place. Use
the long tail of yarn left and stitch
to the base of the muzzle, pulling
it firmly to form the bear's mouth.

Embroider the eyes using black
and white yarn. Sew the ears
together in pairs and attach to either
side of the head. Sew the arm
seams, leaving the tops open for
stuffing. Attach the arms to the
shoulders on either side.

Sew the leg seams and stuff,
ensuring you fill out the feet to give
a nice shape. Sew the legs to each
side of the bear in a sitting position.

Sweater & bandana

Sweater body
make 2

Using 4mm needles and C, cast on 36 sts.

Work 6 rows in k2, p2 rib.

Change to st st and work 30 rows.

Work 6 rows k2, p2 rib.

Cast off.

Sleeves
make 2

Using 4mm needles and C, cast on 30 sts.

Work 5 rows in k2, p2 rib.

Change to st st and work 20 rows.

Cast off.

To make up

Sew the shoulder seams of the sweater body back and front, overlapping the rib from front to back on either side for ¾in (2cm) to form the envelope neck. Now sew the sleeves in position on either side then sew the underarm and side seams. Slip onto the bear.

Bandana
worked in garter stitch

Using 4mm needles and C, cast on 2 sts.

Next row: K1, inc in next st (3 sts).

Next row: Knit.

** **Next row:** Inc in first and last st (5 sts).

Next row: Knit.

Next row: Inc in first and last st (7 sts).

Next row: Knit. **

Knit 16 rows.

K2tog at each end of next and following alt rows (3 sts).

Knit 5 rows.

Work from ** to ** (7 sts).

Cont in garter stitch until strip is long enough to fit around bear's head.

Next row: K2tog at each end of row.

Next row: Knit.

Repeat last 2 rows until you have 3 sts.

Knit 5 rows.

Inc 1 st at each end of next and following alt rows to 7 sts.

Knit 16 rows.

K2tog at each end of next and following alt rows to 3 sts.

Next row: K3tog and fasten off.

Sew in yarn ends and tie around bear's head.

Patches

With his endearing expression and checked shirt, this country bear is all set to melt your heart. Worked in stocking stitch and garter stitch, he is very simple to make. His jumper is embroidered using chain stitch, but it could also be left plain or striped.

. . . .

YOU WILL NEED

For Patches

Bergère de France Norvège, 40% wool, 40% acrylic, 20% mohair (154yds/140m per 50g ball): 2 x 50g balls in 31126 Duvet (A)

Needles size 4mm (UK8:US6)
Needles size 4.5mm (UK7:US7)
Safety stuffing

For the top and dungarees

Sirdar Snuggly DK, 55% nylon, 45% acrylic (179 yds/164m per 50g):
1 x 50g ball Cream shade 203 (B)
1 x 50g ball Denim Blue shade 326 (C)
1 x 50g ball Cherry Pie Shade 437 (D)
Oddments of medium brown, black and white DK yarn for nose and features

Needles size 4mm (UK8:US6)
Shirring elastic

KNITTING NOTES

Tension

20 sts x 26 rows to 4in (10cm) for Norvège using 4.5mm (UK7:US7) needles.
22 sts x 28 rows to 4in (10cm) for DK using 4mm (UK7:US7) needles.

Yarn notes

You may substitute this yarn for a similar weight DK yarn that gives the same tension.

Measurements

11in (28cm) tall when sitting. Circumference of tummy when stuffed is about 15in (38cm).

Abbreviations

Refer to page 33.

Muzzle

Using 4.5mm needles and A, cast on 10 sts.

Next row: Purl.

Next row: Inc in each st across row (20 sts).

Next row: Purl.

Next row: *K1, inc in next st; rep from * to end (30 sts).

Next row: Purl.

Next row: *K2, inc in next st; rep from * to end (40 sts).

Next row: Purl.

Next row: *K3, inc in next st; rep from * to end (50 sts).

Next row: Purl.

Next row: *K4, inc in next st; rep from * to end (60 sts).

Next row: Purl.

Next row: *K5, inc in next st; rep from * to end (70 sts).

Work 6 rows in st st and cast off.

Patches
Body and head
made all in one piece

Using 4.5mm needles and A, cast on 20 sts.

Next row: Purl.

Next row: Inc in each st across row (40 sts).

Next row: Purl.

Next row: *K1, inc in next st; rep from * to end (60 sts).

Cont in st st without further increases for 38 more rows.

Decrease row (mark this row for neck of bear)

Next row: *K4, skpo; rep from * to end (50 sts).

Next row: Purl.

Cont in st st on these 50 sts for a further 26 rows.

Shape top of head

Next row: *K5, skpo; rep from * to last st, k1 (43 sts).

Next and following alt rows: Purl.

Next row: *K4, skpo; rep from * to last st, k1 (36 sts).

Next row: *K3, skpo; rep from * to last st, k1 (29 sts).

Next row: *K2, skpo; rep from * to last st, k1 (22 sts).

Next row: *K1, skpo; rep from * to last st, k1 (15 sts).

Next row: Skpo; rep to last st, k1 (8 sts).

Purl 1 row and cast off.

Right arm

Using 4.5mm needles and A, cast on 10 sts.

Next row: Purl.

Next row: *K1, inc in next st; rep from * across row (15 sts).

Next row: Purl.

Next row: *K1, inc in next st; rep from * to last st, k1 (22 sts).

Next row: Purl.

Next row: Inc in first and last st (24 sts).

Beg with a purl row, work 17 rows in st st.

Shape arm

Next row: K12, turn and purl back.

Next row: K13, turn and purl back.

Next row: K14, turn and purl back.

Next row: K15, turn and purl back.

Next row: Knit across all sts.

Next row: Purl.

Work 8 rows in st st.

Next row: *K1, skpo; rep from * to end (16 sts).

Next row: Purl.

Next row: K2tog across row (8 sts).

Next row: Purl.

Next row: K2tog across row (4 sts).

Break yarn and run through sts left on needle. Draw up and fasten off.

Left arm

Using 4.5mm needles and A, cast on 10 sts.

Next row: Purl.

Next row: *K1, inc in next st; rep from * across row (15 sts).

Next row: Purl.

Next row: *K1, inc in next st; rep from * to last st, k1 (22 sts).

Next row: Purl.

Next row: Inc in first and last st (24 sts).

Beg with a purl row, work 18 rows in st st.

Shape arm

Next row: P12, turn and knit back.

Next row: P13, turn and knit back.

Next row: P14, turn and knit back.

Next row: P15, turn and knit back.

Next row: Purl across all sts.

Work 8 rows in st st.

Next row: *K1, skpo; rep from * to end (16 sts).

Next row: Purl.

Next row: K2tog across row (8 sts).

Next row: Purl.

Next row: K2tog across row (4 sts).

Break yarn and run through sts left on needle. Draw up and fasten off.

Legs
make 2
Using 4.5mm needles and A, cast on 10 sts.

Next row: Purl.

Next row: *K1, inc in next st; rep from * across row (15 sts).

Next row: Purl.

Next row: *K1, inc in next st; rep from * to last st, k1 (22 sts).

Next row: Purl.

Next row: Inc in first and last st (24 sts).

Next row: Purl.

Repeat last 2 rows once more (26 sts).

Cont in st st for 24 rows.

Increase for foot

Next row: K9, inc in each of next 8 sts, k9 (34 sts).

Beg with a purl row, work 11 rows st st.

Next row: K2tog across row (17 sts).

Next row: Purl.

Next row: K2tog across row to last st, k1 (9 sts).

Next row: Purl.

Break yarn and run through sts left on needle. Draw up and fasten off.

Ears
make 4
Using 4.5mm needles and A, cast on 8 sts.

Work in st st for 4 rows.

Next: Inc 1 st at each end of next and following alt rows until you have 14 sts, ending on a purl row. Work 8 rows st st.

Next row: K2tog across row (7 sts).

Cast off.

Nose
worked in garter stitch
Using 4mm needles and medium brown DK yarn, cast on 3 sts and knit 1 row.

Next row: Inc in first and last st (5 sts).

Next row: Knit.

Repeat last 2 rows once more (7 sts).

Knit 6 rows without shaping.

Next row: K2tog at each end of row (5 sts).

Next row: Knit.

Repeat last 2 rows once more.

Knit 1 row and cast off.

To make up

Begin with the head and body of the bear. Sew the seam, which runs down the back of the bear. Leave the base open to stuff. Stuff the head first, making it nice and firm and round. Now take a needle threaded with matching yarn and, beginning at the marked row for the neck, weave the yarn in and out of each stitch all the way around, starting and ending at the seam. Pull up quite firmly to form the head and neck. Secure well at the seam. Continue to stuff the body, then close the base.

Sew the side seam of the muzzle to form a cup shape. Add some stuffing then pin to the front of the bear's head, using the photos as a guide. Sew the muzzle in place. Pin the nose in the centre of the muzzle, so that the longest sides are at the top and bottom. Sew the nose in place. Embroider the eyes and eyebrows using black and white yarn. Sew the ears together in pairs and attach to either side of the head.

Sew the seams on the arms, leaving the top open for stuffing, then attach to the bear's shoulders on either side.

Sew the leg seams and stuff, making sure that you fill out the feet to give a nice shape. Sew the legs to each side of the bear in a sitting position.

Dungarees
Front
**** Begin with first leg.
** Using 4mm needles and C, cast on 23 sts.
Work 2 rows in garter stitch.
Change to st st and work 26 rows.**

Inc for crotch
Next row: Inc 1 st at beginning of row, knit to end.
Next row: Purl to last st, inc in st.
Rep last 2 rows 2 times more (29 sts).
Leave stitches on a spare needle for now.

Work second leg
Work as first leg from ** to **.
Next row: Knit to last st, inc in st.
Next row: Inc in first stitch, purl to end.
Repeat last 2 rows 2 times more.
Join two sets of stitches together
Knit across stitches on needle, now knit across stitches on spare needle (58 sts).
Beg with a purl row, work 21 rows st st on these sts.
Change to k1, p1 rib and work 6 rows. ****

Begin bib
Next row: Cast off 20 sts, k18, cast off 20 sts. Break yarn.
Rejoin yarn to remaining sts and proceed as follows:
Next row: K2, purl to last 2 sts, k2.
Next row: Knit.

Next row: K2, purl to last 2 sts, k2.
Repeat last 2 rows 5 times more.
Knit 4 rows garter stitch across
all stitches.
Next row: K4, cast off 10 sts, k4.
Proceed on first set of 4 sts
for strap.
Knit 46 rows garter stitch and
cast off.
Rejoin yarn to remaining stitches
and work to match first side.

Back

Work as front from **** to **** and
cast off in rib.

Patch

Using 4mm needles and D, cast on
10 sts.
Work in st st for 14 rows and cast off.

To make up

Join the side seams and underleg
seams. Using some shirring elastic
and a blunt-ended needle, thread
elastic through the last 3 rows of the
rib on the back of the dungarees
at waist level. Draw in quite firmly
to take up fullness but maintain
elasticity too. Make sure you fasten
off firmly. Join the straps to the back
edge of the dungarees. Stitch the
patch to one of the legs using a
contrast yarn and large stitches.

Top

Back

Using 4mm needles and B, cast on
37 sts.
Work 3 rows garter stitch.
Change to st st and stripe pattern.
Work 4 rows st st in B.
Join in D yarn.
Work 2 rows st st.
Repeat last 6 rows 5 times more.
Knit 4 rows st st in B.
Work 3 rows garter stitch and
cast off.

Front

Work as back until 4th D stripe is
completed.
Divide for neck
Next row: Knit 18, cast off 1 st, k18.
Proceed on first set of 18 sts for
right front neck.
Next row: Purl to last 2 sts, k2.
Next row: Knit.
Next row: Purl to last 2 sts, k2.
Next row: Using D, knit.
Next row: Using D, purl to last 2
sts, k2.
Next row: Using B, cast off 6 sts,
knit to end.
Next row: Purl to last st, k1.
Continue on these sts, keeping
stripe pattern correct and 1 st in
garter stitch at neck edge until
work matches back.
Work 4 rows garter stitch and
cast off.

Rejoin yarn to sts left and
work to match other side,
reversing shapings.

Sleeves
make 2
Using 4mm needles
and B, cast on 31 sts.
Work 3 rows garter stitch.
Change to st st and stripe pattern
Work 4 rows st st in B.
Join in D yarn.
Work 2 rows st st.
Repeat last 6 rows twice more.
Knit 4 rows st st in B and cast off.

To make up

Using D and a blunt-ended needle,
work chain stitch along the vertical
rows of stocking stitch on each
separate piece of the top. Start from
the centre stitch and miss 3 stitches
of stocking stitch between each
stripe. This is very time consuming
so be patient. Work in the yarn ends
at each stripe.

Now sew the shoulder seams
for approx ¾in (2cm), then join the
sleeves to back and fronts on either
side. Sew the side and sleeve
seams matching the stripes. Make
a twisted cord using D and lace
through the fronts to enable you
to tie the neck.

Pumpkin

Knit this gorgeous Halloween bear to take along with you trick or treating. He even has his own scary cape complete with pumpkin motif. Knitted in stocking stitch, this is a very simple bear to make.

YOU WILL NEED

For Pumpkin
Sirdar Country Style DK, 40% nylon, 30% wool, 30% acrylic (170yds/155m per 50g ball):
2 x 50g balls in 618 Snapdragon (A)

Needles size 4mm (UK8:US6)
Needles size 3.25mm (UK10:US3)
Safety stuffing

For the cape, inner ears and paw pads
Sirdar Country Style DK, 40% nylon, 30% wool, 30% acrylic (170 yds/155m per 50g ball):
2 x 50g balls in 417 Black (B)
Small amounts of green and orange 4-ply yarns for pumpkin motif

Needles size 4mm (UK8:US6)

KNITTING NOTES

Tension
22 sts x 28 rows to 4in (10cm) using 4mm (UK8:US6) needles.

Yarn notes
Any DK weight yarn will work with this project. Check your tension beforehand and change the needle size if needed.

Measurements
10in (26cm) tall when sitting. Circumference of tummy when stuffed is about 13½in (34.5cm).

Abbreviations
Refer to page 33.

Pumpkin

Head

Using 4mm needles and A, cast on 8 sts.

Next row: Purl.

Next row: Inc in each st across row (16 sts).

Next row: Purl.

Next row: K4, m1, k8, m1, k4 (18 sts).

Next row: Purl.

Next row: K4, m1, k1, m1, k8, m1, k1, m1, k4 (22 sts).

Next row: Purl.

Next row: K5, m1, k1, m1, k10, m1, k1, m1, k5 (26 sts).

Cont increasing in this manner, working 2 more stitches between the 2nd and 3rd increases and working a plain purl row between the increase rows, until you have 66 sts, ending on a purl row.

Work 10 rows in st st decreasing 1 st at either end of row on the final row (64 sts).

Decrease for back of head

Next row: *K6, k2tog; rep from * to end (56 sts).

Next and following alt rows: Purl.

Next row: *K5, k2tog; rep from * to end (48 sts).

Next row: *K4, k2tog; rep from * to end (40 sts).

Next row: *K3, k2tog; rep from * to end (32 sts).

Next row: *K2, k2tog; rep from * to end (24 sts).

Next row: *K1, k2tog; rep from * to end (16 sts).

Next row: K2tog across row. Break yarn and run through sts left on needle. Draw up and fasten off.

Body

Using 4mm needles and A, cast on 20 sts.

Next row: Purl.

Next row: Inc in each st across row (40 sts).

Next row: Purl.

Next row: *K1, inc in next st; rep from * to end (60 sts).

Cont in st st without further increases until you have worked 57 rows, ending with a purl row.

Decrease for top of body

Next row: *K4, k2tog; rep from * to end (50 sts).

Next and following alt rows: Purl.

Next row: *K3, k2tog; rep from * to end (40 sts).

Next row: *K2, k2tog; rep from * to end (30 sts).

Next row: *K1, k2tog; rep from * to end (20 sts).

Next row: K2tog across row (10 sts). Break yarn and run through sts left on needle. Draw up and fasten off.

Ears
make 2 in A and 2 in B

Using 4mm needles and appropriate colour, cast on 10 sts.
Work in garter stitch for 2 rows.
Next: Inc in first and last st every alt row to 16 sts.
Work 8 rows garter st.
Next row: K2tog across row.
Next row: Knit.
Next row: K2tog across row.
Cast off.

Arms
make 2

Using 4mm needles and A, cast on 10 sts.
Next row: Purl.
Next row: *K1, inc in next st; rep from * across row (15 sts).
Next row: Purl.
Next row: *K1, inc in next st; rep from * to last st, k1 (22 sts).
Next row: Purl.
Next row: Inc in first and last st (24 sts).
Beg with a purl row, work 27 rows in st st.
Next row: *K1, skpo; rep from * to end (16 sts).
Next row: Purl.
Next row: K2tog across row (8 sts).
Next row: Purl.
Next row: K2tog across row (4 sts).
Break yarn and run through sts left on needle. Draw up and fasten off.

Legs
make 2

Using 4mm needles and A, cast on 10 sts.

Next row: Purl.

Next row: *K1, inc in next st; rep from * across row (15 sts).

Next row: Purl.

Next row: *K1, inc in next st; rep from * to last st, k1 (22 sts).

Next row: Purl.

Next row: Inc in first and last st (24 sts).

Next row: Purl.

Repeat last 2 rows once more (26 sts).

Cont in st st for 24 rows.

Increase for foot

Next row: K9, inc in each of next 8 sts, k9 (34 sts).

Next row: Purl.

Next row: K12, inc in each of next 10 sts, k12 (44 sts).

Beg with a purl row, work 9 rows st st.

Next row: K2tog across row (22 sts).

Next row: Purl.

Next row: K2tog across row (11 sts).

Next row: Purl.

Next row: K2tog across row to last st, k1 (6 sts).

Break yarn and run through sts left on needle. Draw up and fasten off.

Paw pads
make 2, worked in garter stitch

Using 4mm needles and B, cast on 10 sts.

Knit 10 rows.

Next row: K2tog at each end of row.

Next row: Knit.

Repeat last 2 rows until 4 sts remain.

Cast off.

Feet pads
make 2, worked in garter stitch
Using 4mm needles and B, cast on
7 sts.
Knit 2 rows.
Inc 1 st at each end of next and
following alt rows until you have
13 sts.
Knit 12 rows.
Dec 1 st at each end of the next
and following alt rows until you
have 7 sts.
Cast off.

Nose
Using 4mm needles and B, cast on
8 sts.
Work 6 rows in garter stitch.
Now dec 1 st at each end of next
and following alt rows to 2 sts.
Next row: K2tog, fasten off, leaving
a long tail of yarn.

To make up
Sew the seam on the body, which
runs down the back, and stuff
firmly before closing.

Sew the head seam, stuffing
firmly as with the body.

Sew the ears together in pairs,
one black and one orange, curling
them inwards as you do. Sew to
either side of the head.

Take the nose and pin it in place
on the bear's face, pad it out a little
before stitching it in place. Using
black yarn, embroider the eyes onto
the face, tug them a little to create
indentations and add shape to nose.
Attach the bear's head to the body.

Sew the seams on the arms
and legs, all seams run on the
underside of the pieces. Stuff fairly
firmly. Sew a pad to each paw and
a foot pad to the base of each foot.

Pin the limbs in position on the
bear, noting that he is in a sitting
position. Try to get the limbs all
equal so the bear will sit nicely.
Sew in place.

Cape

Using 4mm needles and B, cast on 48 sts.

Work 4 rows in garter stitch.

Next row: K4, purl to last 4 sts, k4.

Next row: Knit.

Next row: K4, purl to last 4 sts, k4.
Repeat last 2 rows twice more.

Next row (make eyelet holes):
K5, *yfwd, k2tog, k1; rep from * to last 5 sts, k5.

Next row: K4, purl to last 4 sts, k4.
Work 4 rows in st st (dec 1 st on last row) (47 sts).

Now begin to shape cape

Next row: K4, *k9, m1, k1, m1; rep from * to last 13 sts, k13 (53 sts).

**Next row: K4, purl to last 4 sts, k4.

Next row: Knit.

Next row: K4, purl to last 4 sts, k4.**

Next row: K14, m1, k1, m1, *k11, m1, k1, m1; rep from * to last 14 sts, k14 (59 sts).
Work from ** to **.

Next row: K15, m1, k1, m1, *k13, m1, k1, m1; rep from * to last 15 sts, k15 (65 sts).
Work from ** to **.
Cont to increase as set until you have worked the row:
"K18, m1, k1, m1, *k19, m1, k1, m1; rep from * to last 18 sts, k18 (83 sts)."

Next row: K4, purl to last 4 sts, k4.

Next row: Knit.

Next row: K4, purl to last 4 sts, k4.
Repeat last 2 rows 7 times more.
Work 5 rows in garter stitch.
Cast off.

To make up

Make a twisted cord using black yarn and thread it through the holes at the neckline. Sew leaves to top of pumpkin. Embroider the eyes and mouth with black yarn. Attach the motif to centre back of cape.

Motif for cape

Pumpkin

Using 3.25mm needles and orange yarn, cast on 10 sts.
Knit 2 rows in garter stitch.
Inc 1 st at each of next and following alt rows to 20 sts.
Work in garter stitch on these sts for 16 rows.
Now decrease 1 st at each end of next and following alt rows to 14 sts.
Knit 2 rows and cast off.

Leaves

Using 3.25mm needles and green 4-ply yarn, cast on 2sts.
Next row: Knit.
**Next row: Inc in first and last stitch (4 sts).
Next row: Knit
Repeat last 2 rows once more (6 sts).
Next row: K2tog at each end of next and following alt row
(2 sts). **
Knit 2 rows.
Work from ** to **.
K2tog and fasten off.

Snowflake

Wrapped up warm in his scarf and earmuffs, this winter bear is all ready to join you for a walk in the snow. You don't have to use the colour I have chosen for his earmuffs and scarf; instead, why not knit them in your own favourite shades?

●●

YOU WILL NEED

For Snowflake

Jarol Heritage DK, 55% wool, 25% acrylic, 20% nylon (270yds/250m per 100g ball): 2 x 100g balls in 100 Cream (A)
Oddment of black DK yarn for features

Needles size 4mm (UK8:US6)
Safety stuffing

For the scarf and earmuffs

Patons Diploma Gold DK 100% wool (98yds/90m per 50g ball):
1 x 50g ball in in 06243 Bright Aqua (B)

Needles size 4mm (UK8:US6)
Pompom maker or small piece of card

KNITTING NOTES

Tension

22 sts x 28 rows to 4in (10cm) using 4mm (UK8:US6) needles.

Yarn notes

Any DK weight yarn will work with this project. Check your tension beforehand and change needle size if needed.

Measurements

10in (26cm) tall when sitting. Circumference of tummy when stuffed is about 13½in (34.5cm).

Abbreviations

Refer to page 33.

Snowflake

Head

Using 4mm needles and A, cast on 8 sts.

Next row: Purl.

Next row: Inc in each st across row (16 sts).

Next row: Purl.

Next row: K4, m1, k8, m1, k4 (18 sts).

Next row: Purl.

Next row: K4, m1, k1, m1, k8, m1, k1, m1, k4 (22 sts).

Next row: Purl.

Next row: K5, m1, k1, m1, k10, m1, k1, m1, k5 (26 sts).

Next row: Purl.

Cont increasing in this manner, working 2 more stitches between the 2nd and 3rd increases and working a plain purl row between the increase rows, until you have 66 sts, ending on a purl row.

Work 10 rows in St st decreasing 1 st at each end of row on the final row (64 sts).

Decrease for back of head

Next row: * K6, k2tog; rep from * to end (56 sts).

Next and following alt rows, purl.

Next row: * K5, k2tog; rep from * to end (48 sts).

Next row: * K4, k2tog; rep from * to end (40 sts).

Next row: * K3, k2tog; rep from * to end (32 sts).

Next row: * K2, k2tog; rep from * to end (24 sts).

Next row: * K1, k2tog; rep from * to end (16 sts).

Next row: K2tog across row (8 sts). Break yarn and run through sts left on needle. Draw up and fasten off.

Body

Using 4mm needles and A, cast on 20 sts.

Next row: Purl.

Next row: Inc in each st across row (40 sts).

Next row: Purl.

Next row: *K1, inc in next st; rep from * to end (60 sts).

Cont in st st without further increases until you have worked 46 more rows.

Decrease for top of body

Next row: *K4, k2tog; rep from * to end (50 sts).

Next and following alt rows:
Purl.

Next row: *K3, k2tog; rep from * to end (40 sts).

Next row: *K2, k2tog; rep from * to end (30 sts).

Next row: *K1, k2tog; rep from * to end (20 sts).

Next row: K2tog across row (10 sts).

Break yarn and run through sts left on needle. Draw up and fasten off.

Ears
make 4

Using 4mm needles and A, cast on 10 sts.

Beg knit work 2 rows st st.

Inc in first and last st on every alt row to 16 sts.

Beg with a purl row, work 5 rows in st st.

Next row: K2tog across row (8 sts).

Next row: Purl.

Next row: K2tog across row (4 sts).

Cast off.

Right arm

Using 4mm needles and A, cast on 10 sts.

Next row: Purl.

Next row: *K1, inc in next st; rep from * across row (15 sts).

Next row: Purl.

Next row: *K1, inc in next st; rep from * to last st, k1 (22 sts).

Next row: Purl.

Next row: Inc in first and last st (24 sts).

Beg with a purl row, work 17 rows in st st.

Shape arm

Next row: K12, turn and purl back.

Next row: K13, turn and purl back.

Next row: K14, turn and purl back.

Next row: K15, turn and purl back.

Next row: Knit across all sts.

Next row: Purl.

Work 8 rows in st st.

Next row: *K1, skpo; rep from * to end (16 sts).

Next row: Purl.

Next row: K2tog across row (8 sts).

Next row: Purl.

Break yarn and run through sts left on needle. Draw up and fasten off.

Left arm

Using 4mm needles and A, cast on 10 sts.

Next row: Purl.

Next row: *K1, inc in next st; rep from * across row (15 sts).

Next row: Purl.

Next row: *K1, inc in next st; rep from * to last st, k1 (22 sts).

Next row: Purl.

Next row: Inc in first and last st (24 sts).

Beg with a purl row, work 18 rows in st st.

Shape arm

Next row: P12, turn and knit back.

Next row: P13, turn and knit back.

Next row: P14, turn and knit back.

Next row: P15, turn and knit back.

Next row: Purl across all sts.

Now work 8 rows in st st.

Next row: *K1, skpo; rep from * to end (16 sts).

Next row: Purl.

Next row: K2tog across row (8 sts).

Next row: Purl.

Next row: K2tog across row (4 sts).

Break yarn and run through sts left on needle. Draw up and fasten off.

Legs

make 2

Using 4mm needles and A, cast on 10 sts.

Next row: Purl.

Next row: *K1, inc in next st; rep from * across row (15 sts).

Next row: Purl.

Next row: *K1, inc in next st; rep from * to last st, k1 (22 sts).

Next row: Purl.

Next row: Inc in first and last st (24 sts).

Next row: Purl.

Repeat last 2 rows once more (26 sts).

Cont in st st for 24 rows.

Increase for foot

Next row: K9, inc in each of next 8 sts, k9 (34 sts).

Next row: Purl.

Next row: K12, inc in each of next 10 sts, k12 (44 sts).

Beg with a purl row, work 9 rows st st.

Next row: K2tog across row (22 sts).

Next row: Purl.

Next row: K2tog across row (11 sts).

Next row: Purl.

Next row: K2tog across row to last st, k1 (6 sts).

Break yarn and run through sts left on needle. Draw up and fasten off.

Nose

Using 4mm needles and black
yarn, cast on 8 sts.
Work 4 rows in st st.
Next row: K2tog, work to last 2 sts,
K2tog (6 sts).
Next row: Purl.
Next row: K2tog, k2, k2tog (4 sts).
Next row: Purl.
Next row: K2tog twice.
Next row: Purl.
Next row: K2tog and fasten off.
Leave a long tail of yarn as you will
use this to form the bear's mouth.

To make up

Sew seam on body, which runs
down the back, and stuff firmly
before closing. Sew seam on the
head, stuffing firmly.

Sew the ears together in pairs,
curling them inwards as you do.
Sew the ears to either side of
the head.

Pin the nose in place on the
bear's face, padding it out a little
with stuffing before stitching in
place. Using some black yarn,
embroider the eyes. Tug them a
little to create indentations and add
shape to the nose. Attach the head
to the body.

Sew the seams on the arms and
legs. Stuff fairly firmly.

Pin the limbs in position on the
bear, noting that he is in a sitting
position and making sure the seams
run on the underside. Try to get
the limbs all equal so the bear
will sit nicely. Sew the arms and
legs in place.

Scarf

Using 4mm needles and B, cast on 13 sts.

Work 4 rows garter stitch.

Begin pattern

Row 1: K6, p1, K6.

Row 2: K3, p3, k1, p3, k3.

Repeat last 2 rows once and then row 1 again.

Next row: Knit.

These 6 rows form pattern.

Rep 5 times more.

Next row: K4, k2tog, k1, k2tog, k4 (11 sts).

Next row: Knit.

Next row: K3, k2tog 3 times, k2 (8 sts).

Next row: Knit.

Next row: K2, k2tog twice, k2 (6 sts).

Knit 60 rows.

Next row: K2, inc in each of next 2 sts, k2 (8 sts).

Next row: Knit.

Next row: K3, inc in each of next 3 sts, k2 (11 sts).

Next row: Knit.

Next row: K4, inc in next st, k1, inc in next st, k4 (13 sts).

Next row: Knit.

Begin pattern

Row 1: K6, p1, K6.

Row 2: K3, p3, k1, p3, k3.

Rep last 2 rows once and then row 1 again.

Next row: Knit.

These 6 rows form pattern.

Repeat pattern rows 5 times more.

Work 4 rows in garter stitch and cast off.

Work in the yarn ends, then wrap around the bear's neck.

Earmuffs

make 2, worked in garter stitch

Using 4mm needles and B, cast on
4 sts.

Knit 2 rows.

Next row: Inc in first and last stitch
(6 sts).

Next row: Knit.

Rep last 2 rows once more (8 sts).

Knit 6 rows.

Next row: K2tog at each end of row
(6 sts).

Next row: Knit.

Rep last 2 rows once more (4 sts).

Knit 2 rows and cast off.

Headband

Using 4mm needles and B, cast
on 28 sts.

Knit 3 rows and cast off.

To make up

To assemble the earmuffs, join
the two circles to either end of the
headband. Make two pompoms
(see below) and trim to a neat
shape. Sew one to each of the
circles. Catch the muffs in place
over the top of the head.

Pompoms can be made using
the clever pompom makers now
available, but they can also
be homemade in the traditional
way using two circles of card with
a hole cut out of the centres, and
winding the yarn around the card
until the centre circle is full. The
yarn is then cut in-between the two
pieces of card and a length of yarn
passed into the same place and
tied tightly. The card is then pulled
away from the resulting pompom,
which will then need to be trimmed
to a neat shape.

Lily

Celebrate a special birthday with this sweet teddy bear! Knitted in a soft furry yarn and with a pretty dress complete with heart motif, Lily will be a joy to own. She has her own birthday cake to knit too, as well as a headband with lovely ribbon roses.

YOU WILL NEED

For Lily
Bergère de France Plume, 47% polyamide, 42% acrylic, 11% wool (65yds/60m per 50g): 2 x 50g balls in 29274 Beige (A)
Bergère de France Norvège, 40% wool, 40% acrylic, 20% mohair (154yds/140m per 50g ball): 1 x 50g ball in 31126 Duvet (B)
Oddment of dark brown yarn for features

Needles size 4.5mm (UK7:US7)
Safety stuffing

For the dress
Sirdar Snuggly DK, 55% nylon, 45% acrylic (179yds/165m per 50g ball):
1 x 50g ball in 199 Trendy Pink (C)
1 x 50g ball in 251 White (D)

Needles size 4mm (UK8:US6)
Small length of pale pink baby ribbon

For the accessories
Small amounts of cream, pale pink, deep pink and yellow DK yarn

Needles size 4mm (UK8:US6)
Cardboard tube 11in (27cm) diameter, 2½in (6cm) depth
Small piece of card to make candle
Safety stuffing and craft glue
9 pink ribbon roses
Piece of green and white spotted ribbon

KNITTING NOTES

Tension
15 sts x 20 rows to 4in (10cm) for Bergere de France Plume and Bergère de France Norvège on 4.5mm (UK7:US7) needles.
22 sts x 28 rows to 4in (10cm) for Sirdar Snuggly DK on 4mm (UK8:US6) needles.

Measurements
11in (28cm) tall when sitting. Circumference of tummy when stuffed is about 14in (35.5cm).

Abbreviations
Refer to page 33.

Tip Lily's skirt could be knitted in stocking stitch if you prefer (see Daisy, page 123).

Lily

Body and head

made all in one piece

Using 4.5mm needles and A, cast on 20 sts.

Next row: Purl.

Next row: Inc in each st across row (40 sts).

Next row: Purl.

Next row: *K1, inc in next st; rep from * to end (60 sts).

Cont in st st for 36 more rows.

Decrease row (mark this row for neck of bear)

Next row: *K4, skpo; rep from * to end (50 sts).

Next row: Purl.

Cont on these 50 sts for a further 26 rows.

Shape top of head

Next row: *K5, skpo; rep from * to last st, k1 (43 sts).

Next and following alt rows: Purl.

Next row: *K4, skpo; rep from * to last st, k1 (36 sts).

Next row: *K3, skpo; rep from * to last st, k1 (29 sts).

Next row: *K2, skpo; rep from * to last st, k1 (22 sts).

Next row: *K1, skpo; rep from * to last st, k1 (15 sts).

Next row: Skpo; rep to last st, k1 (8 sts).

Purl 1 row and cast off.

Muzzle

Using 4.5mm needles and B, cast on 8 sts.

Next row: Purl.

Next row: Inc 1 st at each end of row (10 sts).

Next row: Purl.

Repeat last 2 rows until you have 16 sts, ending with a purl row.

Work 8 rows in st st.

Now dec 1 st at each end of next and following alt rows until you have 8 sts.

Work 2 rows st st and cast off.

Ears
make 2 in A and 2 in B
Using 4.5mm needles and A or B, cast on 10 sts.

Work in st st for 2 rows.

Inc in first and last st of every alt row to 16 sts.

Beg with a purl row, work 7 rows in st st.

Next row: K2tog across row (8 sts).

Next row: Purl.

Next row: K2tog across row (4 sts). Cast off.

Arms
make 2
Using 4.5mm needles and A, cast on 10 sts.

Next row: Purl.

Next row: *K1, inc in next st; rep from * across row (15 sts).

Next row: Purl.

Next row: *K1, inc in next st; rep from * to last st, k1 (22 sts).

Next row: Purl.

Next row: Inc in first and last st (24 sts).

Beg with a purl row, work 24 rows in st st.

Next row: *K1, skpo; rep from * to end (16 sts).

Next row: Purl.

Next row: K2tog across row (8 sts).

Next row: Purl.

Next row: K2tog across row (4 sts). Break yarn and run through sts left on needle. Draw up and fasten off.

Legs

make 2

Using 4.5mm needles and A, cast
on 10 sts.

Next row: Purl.

Next row: *K1, inc in next st; rep
from * across row (15 sts).

Next row: Purl.

Next row: *K1, inc in next st; rep
from * to last st, k1 (22 sts).

Next row: Purl.

Next row: Inc in first and last st
(24 sts).

Next row: Purl.

Repeat last 2 rows once more
(26 sts).

Cont in st st for 22 rows.

Increase for foot

Next row: K9, inc in each of next
8 sts, k9 (34 sts).

Beg with a purl row, work 9 rows
st st.

Next row: K2tog across row
(17 sts).

Next row: Purl.

Next row: K2tog across row to last
st, k1 (9 sts).

Next row: Purl.

Break yarn and run through sts left
on needle. Draw up and fasten off.

To make up

Begin with the head and body of
the bear. Sew the seam, which will
run down the back of the bear.
Leave the base open to stuff.

Stuff the head first, making it
nice and firm and round. Now take
a needle threaded with matching
yarn and, beginning at the marked
row for the neck, weave the yarn
in and out of each stitch all the
way around, starting and ending
at the seam. Pull up quite firmly
to form the head and neck. Secure
well at the seam. Continue to stuff
the body, then close the base.

Sew the side seam of the muzzle
to form a cup shape. Add some
stuffing, then pin it to the front of
the head. Use the photos as a
guide. Sew the muzzle in place.
Pin the nose in the centre of the
muzzle with the widest part at the
top. Add a tiny bit of stuffing
to pad it out slightly, then sew in
place. Use the long tail of yarn
left and stitch to the base of the
muzzle, pulling it firmly to form
the bear's mouth.

Embroider the eyes and
eyebrows. Sew the ears together
in pairs and attach to either side
of the head.

Sew the seams on the arms,
leaving the top edge open, and
stuff. Attach to the shoulders of
the bear on either side.

Sew the leg seams and stuff,
making sure that you fill out the feet
to give a nice shape. Sew the legs
to each side in a sitting position.

Dress

Front

Using 4mm needles and C, cast on
73 sts.

Knit 3 rows garter stitch.

Begin pattern: carry on yarn not in use neatly up side of work

Using D:

Row 1 (RS): K1, *K2tog twice, (yfwd, K1) three times, yfwd, (sl 1, K1, psso) twice, K1; rep from * to end.

Row 2: Purl.

Rows 3–6: Repeat last 2 rows twice more.

Rows 7–10: Using C work 4 rows garter stitch.

Repeat rows: 1–10 twice more.

Repeat rows: 1–6 once more.

Next row: * K2tog *, rep from * to * across row (37 sts)

Next row: Using C Knit.

Next row (make holes for ribbon): K2, * yfwd, K2tog,* rep from * to * to last st , K1.

Next row: Knit.

Break C and join in D.

Work 6 rows in st st.

Shape armholes

Cast off 3 sts at beg of next 2 rows (31 sts).

Next row: K1, skpo, knit to last 3 sts, k2tog, k1 (29 sts).

Next row: K1, purl to last st, k1. ***
Repeat the last 2 rows until you have 19 sts. ending on a purl row.

Shape neck

Next row: K1, skpo, k4, turn (leave rem sts on a stitch holder or spare needle).

Next row: P2tog, purl to last st, k1 (5 sts).

Next row: K1, skpo, k2 (4 sts).

Next row: P2tog, p2 (3 sts).

Next row: Skpo, k1 (2 sts).

Next row: P2tog, fasten off.

Return to sts on holder.

Slip centre 5 sts onto holder for centre neck, rejoin yarn to rem sts and complete to match other side, working k2tog instead of skpo.

Back

Work as front to ***.

Next row: K1, skpo, k11, turn (proceed on this set of sts, leave rem sts on a holder).

Next row: K2, purl to last st, k1.

Next row: K1, skpo, knit to end (11 sts).

Next row: K2, purl to last st, k1.

Cont as on last 2 rows until you have 5 sts left. Leave on a stitch holder.

Rejoin yarn to rem sts, cast off 1 st, knit to last 3 sts, k2tog , K1. Now complete to match first side, reversing shapings and working k2tog instead of skpo.

Sleeves

make 2

Using 4mm needles and C, cast on 32 sts.

Work 3 rows in garter st.

Break C and join in D.

Change to st st and work 8 rows.

Shape armholes

Cast off 3 sts at beg of next 2 rows (26 sts).

Next row: Knit.

Next row: K1, purl to last st, k1.

Rep last 2 rows once more.

Next row: K1, skpo, knit to last 3 sts, k2tog, k1 (24 sts).

Next row: K1, purl to last st, k1.

Cont as on last 2 rows until you have 10 sts left.

Cast off.

To make up and neckband

Sew raglan seams on back, front and sleeves. With right side of work facing, using 4mm needles and D and beginning at left back, pick up and knit 5 sts from left back, 10 sts from first sleeve, 5 sts down side of neck, 5 sts from front neck, 5 sts from other side of neck, 10 sts from sleeve and 5 sts from right back (45 sts).

Next row: Knit.

Break D and join in C.

Knit 2 more rows in garter stitch and cast off firmly.

Now you need to embroider the heart onto the front bodice of the skirt using the Swiss-darning method (see page 27). Mark the centre stitch of the front bodice. Beginning on the first row after casting off for the armholes, centre the first stitch of the heart to align with the centre stitch of the body.

Now work the embroidery from the chart.

Sew sleeve and side seams on dress. Attach a small piece of ribbon on either side of the back neck and tie to fasten.

SWISS DARNING CHART (9 sts x 9 rows)

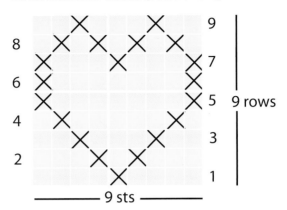

Headband

Using 4mm needles and cream DK, cast on 70 sts.
Knit 4 rows garter st and cast off.

Flower

Using 4mm needles and cream DK, cast on 50 sts.

Next row: Knit.

Next row: K2, *cast off 6 sts, k2; rep from * to end.

Next row: Knit the rem stitches on the needle, thus drawing in the centre of the flower (14 sts). Break yarn leaving a tail end, run the yarn through the remaining stitches, draw up tight and fasten off.

To make up

Join short ends of the headband. Stitch the flower onto the band to cover the join. Sew or glue three ribbon roses to the centre of the flower.

Birthday cake

Side

Using 4mm needles and pale pink DK yarn, cast on 13 sts.

Work in pattern as follows:

Row 1: Knit.

Row 2: Purl.

Row 3: Knit.

Row 4: Knit.

Row 5: Purl.

Row 6: Knit.

Repeat last 6 rows until work is long enough to stretch around cardboard tube.

Top of cake
worked in garter st

Using 4mm needles and cream DK yarn, cast on 9 sts.

Knit 1 row.

Inc 1 st at each end of the next and following alt rows to 17 sts.

Make hole for candle

Next row: K8, cast off 1 st, k8.

Next row: Knit, cast on a stitch over the cast off stitch of previous row.

Knit 4 rows in garter stitch.

Dec 1 st at each end of next and following alt rows to 9 sts.

Cast off.

Candle

Using 4mm needles and deep pink DK yarn, cast on 15 sts.

Knit 10 rows st st.

Cast off.

Flame

Using 4mm needles and yellow DK yarn, cast on 6 sts.

Work 12 rows in st st.

Cast off.

To make up

Join the short ends of the side piece to form a circle. Pin the top piece of the cake inside the circle and sew in place. Slip onto the cardboard tube. Glue in place along the edges. Stuff the inside of the tube to keep the top flat.

Cut a circle of card the same diameter as the tube and place the circle inside the base of the cake to cover the stuffing. Roll a piece of card into a narrow cylinder approx 3in (7.5cm) long to form the candle. Join the candle piece along the side edge, and slip the tube inside.

Fold the flame in half, sew the side seams, place inside the candle tube, then push into the hole made in the top of the cake. This will be a tight fit. Stitch or glue the flame in place.

Take lengths of pale pink and cream yarn and make a twisted cord long enough to fit around the top of the cake. Stitch into a circle, then sew in place. Sew or glue ribbon roses onto the top of the cake. Tie ribbon around the centre of the cake in a big bow.

Sunny

Sunny the panda is all ready to join you for his vacation at the ocean. Wearing trendy striped beach shorts, he is just longing to ride the waves! You can even make him a surfboard to complete his outfit.

• •

YOU WILL NEED

For Sunny

Rico Fashion Fur, 85% acrylic, 15% nylon
(87yds/80m per 50g ball):
2 x 50g balls in 001 Cream (A)
2 x 50g balls in 005 Black (B)
Oddment of black DK yarn for nose

Needles size 5.5mm (UK5:US9)
Needles size 4mm (UK8:US6)
Safety stuffing
1 pair of brown safety eyes

For the shorts and surfboard

Small amounts of Robin DK yarn in neon shades:
Lime 162 (C)
Pink 146 (D)
Lilac 145 (E)
Oddment of black DK yarn for embroidery

Needles size 4mm (UK8:US6)
A piece of plastic canvas or stiff card for
inner surfboard

KNITTING NOTES

Tension

12 sts x 16 rows to 4in (10cm) for Fashion Fur
using 5.5mm (UK5:US9) needles.
22 sts x 28 rows to 4in (10cm) for DK yarn using
4mm (UK8:US6) needles.

Yarn notes

You may substitute the yarns listed for any eyelash
or double knitting weight yarns, but do check your
tension. By substituting the yarns your bear will
not look quite the same as the one in the book and
therefore may be slightly smaller in size.

Measurements

Bear: 11in (28cm) tall when sitting. Circumference
of tummy when stuffed is about 13½in (34.5cm).
Surfboard: 9½in (24cm) tall and 4¼in (11cm) wide.

Abbreviations

Refer to page 33.

Tip It isn't easy to count rows in this type of yarn so take care to mark down the rows as you work.

Sunny

Head

Using 5.5mm needles and A, cast on 10 sts.

Next row: Purl.

Next row: Inc in each stitch across row (20 sts).

Beg with a purl row, work 3 rows st st.

Next row: *K1, inc in next st; repeat from * to end (30 sts).

Beg with a purl row, work 3 rows st st.

Next row: *K1, inc in next st; repeat from * to end (45 sts).

Beg with a purl row, work 11 rows st st.

Shape top of head

Next row: *K1, k2tog; rep from * to end of row (30 sts).

Beg with a purl row, work 3 rows st st.

Next row: K2tog across row (15 sts).

Next row: Purl.

Break yarn and run through sts left on needle. Draw up and fasten off.

Muzzle

Using 5.5mm needles and A, cast on 8 sts.

Next row: Purl.

Next row: Inc in each st across row (16 sts).

Next row: Purl.

Next row: *K1, inc in next st; rep from * to end (24 sts).

Next row: Purl.

Next row: *K2, inc in next st; rep from * to end (32 sts).

Work 3 rows st st.

Next row: *K3, inc in next st; rep from * to end (40 sts).

Work in st st for 5 rows and cast off.

Body

Using 5.5mm needles and A, cast on 10 sts.

Next row: Purl.

Next row: Inc in each stitch across row (20 sts).

Beg with a purl row, work 3 rows st st.

Next row: *K1, inc in next st; rep from * to end (30 sts).

Beg with a purl row, work 3 rows st st.

Next row: *K1, inc in next st; rep from * to end (45 sts).

Beg with a purl row, cont in st st. When work measures 5in (13cm), break A and join in B.

Work in st st for a further 3in (8cm) using B.

Shape top of body

Next row: *K1, k2tog; rep from * to end of row (30 sts).

Beg with a purl row, work 3 rows st st.

Next row: K2tog all across row (15 sts).

Next row: Purl.

Break yarn and run through sts left on needle. Draw up and fasten off.

Legs
make 2

Using 5.5mm needles and B, cast on 8 sts.

Next row: Purl.

Next row: Inc in each st across row (16 sts).

Work 5 rows st st.

Next row: Inc 1 st at each end of row (18 sts).

Work 3 rows st st.

Next row: *K2, inc in next st; rep from * to end (24 sts).

Work 17 rows st st.

Next row: K9, inc in each of next 6 sts, k9 (30 sts).

Next row: Purl.

Next row: K12, inc in each of next 6 sts, k12 (36 sts).

Beg with a purl row, work 5 rows st st.

Next row: K2tog across row (18 sts).

Next row: Purl.

Next row: K2tog across row (9 sts).

Next row: Purl.

Break yarn and run through sts left on needle. Draw up and fasten off.

Arms

make 2

Using 5.5mm needles and B, cast on 8 sts.

Next row: Purl.

Next row: Inc in each st across row (16 sts).

Next row: Purl.

Work 4 rows st st.

Next row: Inc 1 st at each end (18 sts).

Work 13 rows st st.

Next row: *K2, inc in next st; rep from * to end (24 sts).

Work 7 rows st st.

Next row: K2tog across row (12 sts).

Next row: Purl.

Next row: K2tog across row (6 sts).

Next row: Purl.

Break yarn and run through sts left on needle. Draw up and fasten off.

Ears

make 2

Using 5.5mm needles and B, cast on 8 sts.

Next row: Purl.

Next row: Inc in each st across row (16 sts).

Work 5 rows st st.

Next row: K2tog across row (8 sts).

Next row: Purl.

Next row: K2tog across row (4 sts).

Cast off.

Eye patches

make 2

Using 5.5mm needles and B, cast on 6 sts.

Next row: Purl.

Next row: Inc 1 st at each end of row (8 sts).

Next row: Purl.

Work 6 rows in st st.

Next row: Dec 1 st at each end of next and following alt rows until you have 2 sts.

Next row: Purl.

Cast off.

Nose

Using 4mm needles and black DK yarn, cast on 10 sts.

Work 12 rows in garter stitch.

Next row: K2tog at each end of row (8 sts).

Next row: Knit.

Repeat last 2 rows until you have 2 sts.

Cast off.

To make up

The seams run down the back of the head and body, and the undersides of the arms and legs. Sew the body seam first, leaving the cast-on end open for stuffing. Stuff firmly to give a nice rounded shape. Close the gap.

Sew the head in the same way, leaving an opening at the base for stuffing. Stuff partially, as eyes still have to be inserted, and do not close the base yet.

Sew the seams on the arms and, as before, leave the cast-on edge open to enable stuffing. To stuff the arms, push plenty of stuffing down into the paw first then continue stuffing the rest of the arm. Sew the leg seams. Push extra stuffing into the feet to shape.

Sew the muzzle seam; this will run underneath. Pin to the front of the bear's head and add stuffing to give shape. This will take a little time to make it look good. Now sew it onto the face, adding more stuffing to give a good shape. Sew the nose to the centre of the muzzle.

Pin the ears onto the head on either side. Try to get them level. Take some matching yarn and curl the ears into a semi-circular shape, then stitch in place. Sew the eye patches to either side of the bear's head. Take safety eyes and push them through the eye patches, positioning them correctly before snapping on the backs.

Embroider the mouth with black yarn.

Now assemble the bear. Pin his legs in place first, noting he is in the sitting position and making them level if you can. Sew the legs in place. Pin the arms in position as you did with the legs and sew firmly in place. Finally, sew the bear's head onto the body.

Shorts

make 2

Using 4mm needles and C, cast on 40 sts.

Work in k2, p2 rib for 4 rows.

Next row (eyelet holes for cord): *K2, yrn, p2tog; rep from * to end.

Work 3 more rows in k2, p2 rib.

Change to D and work 10 rows st st.

Change to E and work 4 rows st st.

Next row: K19, m1, k2, m1, k19 (42 sts).

Next row: Purl.

Next row: K20, m1, k2, m1, k20 (44 sts).

Next row: Purl.

Divide for legs

Next row: K21, cast off 2 sts, k21. Proceed on first set of sts as follows:

Next row: Purl.

Work 5 rows st st.

Change to garter stitch and work 5 rows. Cast off.

Rejoin yarn to remaining sts and complete to match first leg.

Stripe

Using 4mm needles and black yarn, cast on 36sts.

Work 6 rows garter stitch and cast off.

To make up

Sew the side seams and leg seams. Using lime yarn, make a twisted cord and thread it through the waist. Sew the stripe onto the shorts.

Surfboard

make 2

Using 4mm needles and C, cast on
13 sts, join in E and cast on 13 sts
(26 sts).

Work in stst for 7½in (19cm)
remembering to twist yarns
together on the wrong side of the
work when changing colours to
avoid any holes in the fabric.
Cont in E only (cont in C only
when working the other side).
Work 2 rows st st.

K2tog at each end of next and
following alt rows to 14 sts.
Cast off.

Wristband

Using 4mm needles and lilac DK
yarn, cast on 8 sts.
Knit 34 rows in garter st and
cast off.

To make up

Cut some stiff card or plastic
canvas to measure 9½in (24cm)
in length and 4¼in (11cm) in width.
Round the corners off at one end
for the top of the surfboard.

Sew the seam all around the two
knitted pieces, then turn right sides
out. Slip in the shaped card or
plastic canvas and stretch a little to
give a snug fit. Sew the base closed
neatly. You can embroider a couple
of vertical lines using black yarn or
a number onto one side if you like.

For the wrist band, sew the short
ends together. Make a twisted cord
in lilac and attach to the wristband.
Attach the cord and band to the top
of the surfboard.

Mortimer

Make this earnest bear as a keepsake for a special graduate. You can personalize
the colours to appeal to the recipient, perhaps matching their college colours.
You could even add initials onto the gown with some simple embroidery.

YOU WILL NEED

For Mortimer

Rico Fashion Fur, 85% acrylic, 15% nylon
(87yds/80m per 50g ball):
2 x 50g balls in 003 Brown (A)
1 x 50g ball in medium brown DK (B)
Oddment of black DK yarn for features

Needles size 5.5mm (UK5:US9)
Needles size 4mm (UK8:US6)
Safety stuffing
1 pair of safety eyes

For the gown and accessories

Sirdar Snuggly DK, 55% nylon, 45% acrylic
(179 yds/164m per 50g):
2 x 50g ball Royal Blue (C)
1 x 50g ball Gold (D)
Oddment of White (E)

Needles size 4mm (UK8:US6)
Length of red satin ribbon
4in (10cm) square of stiff card
or plastic canvas

KNITTING NOTES

Tension

12 sts x 16 rows to 4in (10cm) for Fashion Fur using
5.5mm (UK5:US9) needles.
22 sts x 28 rows to 4in (10cm) for DK yarn using
4mm (UK8:US6) needles.

Yarn notes

You may substitute the yarns listed for any eyelash
or double knitting weight yarns, but do check your
tension. By substituting the yarns your bear will
not look quite the same as the one in the book.

Measurements

11in (28cm) tall when sitting. Circumference of
tummy when stuffed is about 13½in (34.5cm).

Abbreviations

Refer to page 33.

Tip It isn't easy to count rows in
this type of yarn so take care
to mark down the rows as you work.

Mortimer

Head

Using 5.5mm needles and A, cast on 10 sts.

Next row: Purl.

Next row: Inc in each stitch across row (20 sts).

Beg with a purl row, work 3 rows st st.

Next row: *K1, inc in next st; repeat from * to end (30 sts).

Beg with a purl row, work 3 rows st st.

Next row: *K1, inc in next st; repeat from * to end (45 sts).

Beg with a purl row, work 11 rows st st.

Shape top of head

Next row: *K1, k2tog; rep from * to end of row (30 sts).

Beg with a purl row, work 3 rows st st.

Next row: K2tog across row (15 sts).

Next row: Purl.

Break yarn and run through sts left on needle. Draw up and fasten off.

Muzzle

Using 4mm needles and B, cast on 8 sts.

Next row: Purl.

Next row: Inc in each st across row (16 sts).

Next row: Purl.

Next row: *K1, inc in next st; rep from * to end (24 sts).

Next row: Purl.

Work 4 rows st st.

Next row: *K1, inc in next st; rep from * to end (36 sts).

Work in st st for 6 rows and cast off.

Nose

Using 4mm needles and black yarn, cast on 8 sts.

Work 4 rows in st st.

Next row: K2tog, work to last 2 sts, k2tog (6 sts).

Next row: Purl.

Next row: K2tog, k2, k2tog (4 sts).

Next row: Purl.

Next row: K2tog twice (2 sts).

Next row: Purl.

Next row: K2tog and fasten off.

Leave a long tail of yarn as you will use this to form the mouth.

Body

Using 5.5mm needles and A, cast on 10 sts.

Next row: Purl.

Next row: Inc in each st across row (20 sts).

Beg with a purl row, work 3 rows st st.

Next row: *K1, inc in next st; rep from * to end (30 sts).

Beg with a purl row, work 3 rows st st.

Next row: *K1, inc in next st; rep from * to end (45 sts).

Beg with a purl row, work 31 rows st st.

Shape top of body

Next row: *K1, k2tog; rep from * to end of row (30 sts).

Beg with a purl row, work 3 rows st st.

Next row: K2tog all across row (15 sts).

Next row: Purl.

Break yarn and run through sts left on needle. Draw up and fasten off.

Legs
make 2

Using 5.5mm needles and A, cast on 8 sts.

Next row: Purl.

Next row: Inc in each st across row (16 sts).

Work in st st for 5 rows.

Next row: Inc 1 st at each end of row (18 sts).

Work 3 rows st st.

Next row: *K2, inc in next st; rep from * to end (24 sts).

Work 11 rows st st.

Next row: *K1, k2tog; rep from * to end (16 sts).

Work 7 rows st st.

Next row: K5, inc in each of next 6 sts, k5 (22 sts).

Next row: Purl.

Next row: K5, (k1, inc1) 6 times, k5 (28 sts).

Work 5 rows st st and cast off fairly loosely.

Arms
make 2

Using 5.5mm needles and A, cast on 8 sts.

Next row: Purl.

Next row: Inc in each st across row (16 sts).

Next row: Purl.

Work 4 rows st st.

Next row: Inc 1 st at each end of row (18 sts).

Work 13 rows st st.

Next row: *K2, inc in next st; rep from * to end (24 sts).

Work 7 rows st st.

Next row: K2tog across row (12 sts).

Next row: Purl.

Next row: K2tog across row (6 sts).

Cast off.

Feet pads
make 2

Using 4mm needles and B, cast on 8 sts.

Next row: Purl.

Inc 1 st at each end of next and following alt rows until you have 14 sts.

Knit 11 rows in st st.

Dec 1 st at each end of next and following alt rows until you have 8 sts.

Cast off.

Ears
make 2

Using 5.5mm needles and A, cast on 8 sts.

Next row: Purl.

Next row: Inc in each st across row (16 sts).

Work 5 rows st st.

Next row: K2tog across row (8 sts).

Next row: Purl.

Next row: K2tog across row (4 sts).

Cast off.

To make up

Sewing up with this type of yarn needs care. Use a big-eyed, blunt-ended needle and short lengths of yarn. Seams will run down the back of the head and body, and the undersides of the arms and legs.

Sew the body seam first, leaving one end open to stuff. Stuff firmly to give a nice rounded shape, then close the gap. Sew the head in the same way, leaving an opening to stuff. Only partially stuff the head as you need to insert the safety eyes before closing the gap. Take the muzzle and sew the seam, which will run underneath. Pin to the front of the head and add stuffing to give shape. Sew the muzzle onto the face, adding more stuffing to give a good shape. Sew the nose in place. Insert the safety eyes on either side of the nose, and click into place. Complete stuffing the head and close the gap.

Pin the ears onto the head on either side. Try to get them level. Take some matching yarn, curl the ears into a semi-circular shape and then stitch in place onto the head. Sew the arm seams and, as before, leave the cast-on edge open to enable stuffing. To stuff the arms, push plenty of stuffing down into the paw then continue stuffing the rest of the arm.

Sew the leg seams and stuff them, noting the base will be left open to enable you to sew on the foot pads. Take a foot pad and pin it in place all around the foot opening,

adding more stuffing if needed. Carefully sew in place all around the opening.

Now assemble the bear. Pin on his legs first, noting he is in the sitting position. Sew them in place, getting them level if you can. Pin and sew the arms in position as you did with the legs. Finally, sew the bear's head onto the body.

Gown

Using 4mm needles and C, cast on 50 sts.

Work 4 rows in garter stitch.

Next row: Knit.

Next row: K4, purl to last 4 sts, k4.

Repeat the last 2 rows 18 times more.

Work 6 rows garter stitch across all stitches.

Divide for fronts

Next row: K20, cast off 10 sts, k20.

First side

Next row: K2tog, knit to end (19 sts).

Next row: K4, purl to last 2 sts, k2.

Next row: K2, k2tog, knit to end (18 sts).

Next row: K4, purl to last 2 sts, k2.

Repeat last 2 rows once more (17 sts).

Work until front matches back, ending on a purl row.

Work 4 rows garter stitch.

Cast off.

Rejoin yarn to remaining stitches and complete to match first side, reversing the shapings.

Sash

make 2

Using 4mm needles and C, cast on 50 sts.

Knit 2 rows garter stitch.

Join in D and commencing with a purl row, dec 1 st at each end of every row for next 5 rows. Break D. Join in C. Work 3 rows garter stitch, still decreasing at each end of every row.

Cast off.

To make up

Fold the gown in half at the shoulders and join the side seams for approx 1¼in (3cm). Join the short ends of the sash, matching the colours. You should have a neat point in the centre of the back and front. Fold the sash in half, matching points to points. Pin one point to the centre back of the gown. Now pin the sash on each side of the shoulders. Fold the sash over both fronts. Catch down either side but leave the point free. Slip the gown onto the bear and arrange the sash to lay flat on either side.

Mortar board

Top

Using 4mm needles and C, cast on 24 sts.
Work in st st for 8in (20cm). Cast off.

Base

Using 4mm needles and C, cast on 11 sts.
Work in garter stitch for 8in (20cm). Cast off.

To make up

Take the top of the mortar board piece and fold in half, then join the two short side seams. Insert a square of stiff card or plastic canvas. Sew up the remaining edge.

Take the base and fold it in half lengthways. Sew the seam. Join into a circle and sew the short ends together. Sew the circle centrally to one side of the top.

Using C, make a twisted chain and tassel (see page 31) and sew to the centre top of the mortar board.

Scroll certificate

Using 4mm needles and E, cast on 26 sts.
Knit 4 rows garter stitch.
Next row: K2, purl to last 2 sts, k2.
Next row: Knit.
Repeat last 2 rows 11 times more.
Work 4 rows garter stitch and cast off.

To make up

Roll the scroll into a cylinder and sew the sides. Tie a piece of red ribbon around the centre of the scroll.

Mr Tubbs

Mr Tubbs is just waiting to be hugged. His faded tweedy look and endearing face will soon melt your heart. He wears a waistcoat to keep out the chills on cooler days. He is a very easy-to-knit bear, using just reverse stocking stitch and garter stitch.

YOU WILL NEED

For Mr Tubbs
James C Brett Marble DK, 100% acrylic
(262yds/240m per 100g ball):
1 x 100g ball in MT8 Autumn (A)
Stylecraft Life DK, 75% acrylic, 25% wool
(326yds/298m per 100g ball):
1 x 100g ball in 2318 Bracken (B)
Oddment of black DK yarn for features

Needles size 4.5mm (UK7:US7)
Needles size 4mm (UK8:US6)
Safety stuffing

For the waistcoat
Stylecraft Life DK, 75% acrylic, 25% wool
(326yds/298m per 100g ball):
1 x 100g ball in 2312 Copper (C)

Needles size 4.5mm (UK7:US7)

KNITTING NOTES

Tension
20 sts x 26 rows to 4in (10cm) using
4.5mm (UK7:US7) needles.

Yarn notes
Any DK weight yarn will work with this project.
Check your tension beforehand and change
needle size if needed.

Measurements
11in (28cm) tall when sitting. Circumference of
tummy when stuffed is about 14in (36cm).

Abbreviations
Refer to page 33.

Mr Tubbs

Body and head

made all in one piece

Using 4.5mm needles and A, cast 20 sts.

Next row: Purl.

Next row: Inc in each st across row (40 sts).

Next row: Purl.

Next row: *K1, inc in next st; rep from * to end (60 sts).

Cont in st st without further increases for 39 more rows.

Decrease row (mark this row for neck of bear)

Next row: *K4, skpo; rep from * to end (50 sts).

Next row: Purl.

Cont in st st on these 50 sts for a further 24 rows.

Shape top of head

Next row: *K5, skpo; rep from * to last st, k1 (43 sts).

Next and following alt rows: Purl.

Next WS row: *K4, skpo; rep from * to last st, k1 (36 sts).

Next WS row: *K3, skpo; rep from * to last st, k1 (29 sts).

Next WS row: *K2, skpo; rep from * to last st, k1 (22 sts).

Next WS row: *K1, skpo; rep from * to last st, k1 (15 sts).

Next WS row: Skpo; rep to last st, k1 (8 sts).

Purl 1 row and cast off.

Muzzle

Using 4mm needles and B, cast on 10 sts.

Next row: Purl.

Next row: Inc in each st across row (20 sts).

Next row: Purl.

Next row: *K1, inc in next st; rep from * to end (30 sts).

Next row: Purl.

Next row: *K2, inc in next st; rep from * to end (40 sts).

Next row: Purl.

Next row: *K3, inc in next st; rep from * to end (50 sts).

Next row: Purl.

Next row: *K4, inc in next st; rep from * to end (60 sts).

Next row: Purl.

Work 4 rows in st st and cast off.

Ears

make 2 in A and 2 in B

Using 4mm needles and A, cast on 10 sts.

Work in st st for 2 rows.

Next row: Inc 1 st at each end of every alt row to 16 sts.

Beg with a purl row, work 5 rows work in st st.

Next row: K2tog across row (8 sts).

Next row: Purl.

Next row: K2tog across row.

Cast off.

Right arm

Using 4.5mm needles and A, cast on 10 sts.

Next row: Purl.

Next row: *K1, inc in next st; rep from * across row (15 sts).

Next row: Purl.

Next row: *K1, inc in next st; rep from * to last st, k1 (22 sts).

Next row: Purl.

Next row: Inc in first and last st (24 sts).

Beg with a purl row, work 17 rows in st st.

Shape arm

Next row: K12, turn and purl back.

Next row: K13, turn and purl back.

Next row: K14, turn and purl back.

Next row: K15, turn and purl back.

Next row: Knit across all sts.

Next row: Purl.

Work 8 rows in st st.

Next row: *K1, skpo; rep from * to end (16 sts).

Next row: Purl.

Next row: K2tog across row (8 sts).

Next row: Purl.

Next row: K2tog across row (4 sts).

Break yarn and run through sts left on needle. Draw up and fasten off.

Left arm

Using 4.5mm needles and A, cast on 10 sts.

Next row: Purl.

Next row: *K1, inc in next st; rep from * across row (15 sts).

Next row: Purl.

Next row: *K1, inc in next st; rep from * to last st, k1 (22 sts).

Next row: Purl.

Next row: Inc in first and last st (24 sts).

Beg with a purl row, work 18 rows in st st.

Shape arm

Next row: P12, turn and knit back.

Next row: P13, turn and knit back.

Next row: P14, turn and knit back.

Next row: P15, turn and knit back.

Next row: Purl across all sts.

Work 8 rows in st st.

Next row: *K1, skpo; rep from * to end (16 sts).

Next row: Purl.

Next row: K2tog across row (8 sts).

Next row: Purl.

Next row: K2tog across row (4 sts).

Break yarn and run through sts left on needle. Draw up and fasten off.

Legs
make 2

Using 4.5mm needles and A, cast on 10 sts.

Next row: Purl.

Next row: *K1, inc in next st; rep from * across row (15 sts).

Next row: Purl.

Next row: *K1, inc in next st; rep from * to last st, k1 (22 sts).

Next row: Purl.

Next row: Inc in first and last st (24 sts).

Next row: Purl.

Repeat last 2 rows once more (26 sts).

Cont in st st for 20 rows.

Increase for foot

Next row: K9, inc in each of next 8 sts, k9 (34 sts).

Beg with a purl row, work 9 rows.

Next row: K2tog across row (17 sts).

Next row: Purl.

Next row: K2tog across row to last st, k1 (9 sts).

Next row: Purl.

Break yarn and run through sts left on needle. Draw up and fasten off.

Nose

Using 4mm needles and black yarn, cast on 8 sts.

Work 4 rows in st st.

Next row: K2tog, work to last 2 sts, k2tog (6 sts).

Next row: Purl.

Next row: K2tog, k2, k2tog (4 sts).

Next row: Purl.

Next row: K2tog twice.

Next row: Purl.

Next row: K2tog and fasten off.

Leave a long tail of yarn as you will use this to form the mouth.

To make up

NOTE The reversed st st is the right side of the fabric, EXCEPT for the muzzle and inner ears which are smooth st st.

Begin with the head and body of the bear. Sew the seam that runs down the back of the bear. Leave the base open to stuff. Stuff the head first, making it nice and firm and round. Now take a needle threaded with matching yarn and, beginning at the marked row for the neck, weave the yarn in and out of each stitch all the way around, starting and ending at the seam. Pull up quite firmly to form the head and neck. Secure well at the seam. Continue to stuff the body, then close the base.

Sew the side seam of the muzzle to form a cup shape. Add some stuffing, then pin it to the front of the bear. Use the photos as a guide. Sew the muzzle in place. Pin the nose in the centre of the muzzle with the widest part at the top.

Add a tiny bit of stuffing to pad it out slightly, then sew in place. Use the long tail of yarn left and stitch to the base of the muzzle, pulling it firmly to form the bear's mouth. Embroider the eyes and eyebrows using black yarn.

Sew the ears together in pairs, with the dark brown ears inside the tweed ears. Attach to either side of the head.

Sew the seams on the arms, leaving the top edge open, and stuff. Attach to the shoulders of the bear on either side. Sew the leg seams and stuff, making sure that you fill out the feet to give a nice shape. Sew the legs to each side in a sitting position.

Waistcoat

Back

Using 4.5mm needles and C, cast on 43 sts.

Work 6 rows in garter stitch.

Begin pattern

Work 4 rows st st.

Work 2 rows in single moss stitch.

These 6 rows form the pattern.

Repeat last 6 rows once more.

Work 2 rows in st st.

Shape armhole, keeping continuity of the pattern

Cast off 4 sts at beg of next 2 rows.

Dec 1 st at each end of next and on following alt rows to 29 sts.

Cont in pattern until you have worked 32 patterned rows in total.

Cast off.

Right front

Using 4.5mm needles and C, cast on 23 sts.

Work 6 rows garter stitch.

Begin pattern

Work 4 rows in st st.

Work 2 rows in single moss stitch.

Repeat last 6 rows once more. **

Work 1 row st st, ending with WS facing for next row.

Shape armhole and neck, keeping continuity of the pattern

Next row: Cast off 4 sts, purl to end.

Now dec 1 st at armhole edge on next and following 3 alt rows and at the same time dec 1 st at front edge on every row until you have 7 sts.

Cont in pattern until front matches back to shoulders.

Cast off.

Left front

Work as right front to **.

Work 2 rows in st st, ending with RS facing for next row.

Shape armhole and neck, keeping continuity of the pattern

Next row: Cast off 4 sts, knit to end.

Next row: Purl.

Now dec 1 st at armhole edge on next and following 3 alt rows and at the same time dec 1 st at front edge on every row until you have 7 sts.

Cont in pattern until front matches back to shoulders.

Cast off.

Button loops
make 2

Using 4.5mm needles and C, cast on 12 sts.
Cast off.

To make up

Sew the side seams of the waistcoat and join the shoulder seams. Sew on the buttons and button loops, overlapping the fronts slightly. Slip on to the bear.

Buttons
make 2

Using 4.5mm needles and C, cast on 3 sts.

Next row: Purl.

Next row: Inc in each st across row (6 sts).

Next row: Purl.

Next row: Inc in each st across row (12 sts).

Next row: Purl.

Break yarn and run through sts on needle, draw up tight to form a circle and secure with a stitch. Join the tiny side seam and form into a tight ball, flatten slightly to form the button shape and secure with a few stitches at base.

Cuddles

What nicer way to snuggle up in bed than with your favourite cuddly bedtime bear! Complete with her own pyjamas that even have a panda motif on the front, she will soon become a much loved night-time companion for any youngster.

● ●

YOU WILL NEED

For Cuddles
Rico Fashion Fur, 85% acrylic, 15% nylon (87yds/80m per 50g ball):
2 x 50g balls Dark Brown (A)
1 x 50g ball mid-brown DK yarn (B)
Oddment of black yarn for features

Needles size 5.5mm (UK5:US9)
Needles size 4mm (UK8:US6) needles
Safety stuffing
1 pair of safety eyes

For the pyjamas
Sirdar Snuggly DK, 55% nylon, 45% acrylic (179yds/165m per 50g):
1 x 50g ball in 443 Pink Plum (C)
1 x 50g ball in 303 Cream (D)
1 x 50g ball in 188 Peaceful (E)
Oddment of black fashion fur or eyelash yarn

Needles size 4mm (UK8:US6) needles
Black embroidery thread
Small ribbon bow

For the slippers and hot-water bottle
Oddments of DK left over from pyjamas
Needles size 4mm (UK8:US6)
Teddy bear sew-on patch for hot-water bottle

KNITTING NOTES

Tension
12 sts x 16 rows to 4in (10cm) for Fashion Fur using 5.5mm (UK5:US9) needles.
22 sts x 28 rows to 4in (10cm) for DK yarn using 4mm (UK8:US6) needles.

Yarn notes
You may substitute the yarns listed for any eyelash or double knitting weight yarns, but do check your tension. By substituting the yarns your bear will not look quite the same as the one in the book and therefore may be slightly smaller in size.

Measurements
11in (28cm) tall when sitting. Circumference of tummy when stuffed is about 14in (35.5cm).

Abbreviations
Refer to page 33.

Tip It isn't easy to count rows in this type of yarn so take care to mark down the rows as you work.

Cuddles

Head

Using 5.5mm needles and A, cast on 10 sts.

Next row: Purl.

Next row: Inc in each stitch across row (20 sts).

Beg with a purl row, work 3 rows st st.

Next row: *K1, inc in next st; repeat from * to end (30 sts).

Beg with a purl row, work 3 rows st st.

Next row: *K1, inc in next st; repeat from * to end (45 sts).

Beg with a purl row, work 11 rows st st.

Shape top of head

Next row: *K1, k2tog; rep from * to end of row (30 sts).

Beg with a purl row, work 3 rows st st.

Next row: K2tog all across row (15 sts).

Next row: Purl.

Next row: K2tog (7 times), K1. Break yarn and run through sts left on needle. Draw up and fasten off.

Muzzle

Using 4mm needles and B, cast on 8 sts.

Next row: Purl.

Next row: Inc in each stitch across row (16 sts).

Next row: Purl.

Next row: *K1, inc in next st; rep from * to end (24 sts).

Next row: Purl.

Next row: *K2, inc in next st; rep from * to end (32 sts).

Work 3 rows st st.

Next row: *K3, inc in next st; rep from * to end (40 sts).

Work in st st for 5 rows and cast off.

Nose

Using 4mm needles and black yarn, cast on 8 sts.

Work 4 rows st st.

Next row: K2tog, work to last 2 sts, k2tog (6 sts).

Next row: Purl.

Next row: K2tog, k2, k2tog (4 sts).

Next row: Purl.

Next row: K2tog twice (2 sts).

Next row: Purl.

Next row: K2tog and fasten off. Leave a long tail of yarn as you will use this to form the mouth.

Body

Using 5.5mm needles and A, cast on 10 sts.

Next row: Purl.

Next row: Inc in each stitch across row (20 sts).

Beg with a purl row, work 3 rows st st.

Next row: *K1, inc in next st; rep from * to end (30 sts).

Beg with a purl row, work 3 rows st st.

Next row: *K1, inc in next st; rep from * to end (45 sts).

Beg with a purl row, work 31 rows st st.

Shape top of body

Next row: *K1, k2tog; rep from * to end of row (30 sts).

Beg with a purl row, work 3 rows st st.

Next row: K2tog across row (15 sts).

Next row: Purl.

Break yarn and run through sts left on needle. Draw up and fasten off.

Legs
make 2

Using 5.5mm needles and A, cast on 8 sts.

Next row: Purl.

Next row: Inc in each st across row (16 sts).

Work in st st for 5 rows.

Next row: Inc 1 st at each end of row (18 sts).

Work 3 rows st st.

Next row: *K2, inc in next st; rep from * to end (24 sts).

Work 17 rows st st.

Next row: K9, inc in each of next 6 sts, k9 (30 sts).

Next row: Purl.

Next row: K12, inc in each of next 6 sts, k12 (36 sts).

Beg with a purl row, work 5 rows st st.

Next row: K2tog across row (18 sts).

Next row: Purl.

Next row: K2tog across row (9 sts).

Next row: Purl.

Break yarn and run through sts left on needle. Draw up and fasten off.

Arms
make 2

Using 5.5mm needles and A, cast on 8 sts.

Next row: Purl.

Next row: Inc in each st across row (16 sts).

Next row: Purl.

Work 4 rows st st.

Next row: Inc 1 st at each end (18 sts).

Work 13 rows st st.

Next row: *K2, inc in next st; rep from * to end (24 sts).

Work 7 rows st st.

Next row: K2tog across row (12 sts).

Next row: Purl.

Next row: K2tog across row (6 sts).

Next row: Purl.

Break yarn and run through sts left on needle. Draw up and fasten off.

Outer ears
make 2

Using 5.5mm needles and A, cast on 8 sts.

Next row: Purl.

Next row: Inc in each st across row (16 sts).

Work 5 rows st st.

Next row: K2tog across row (8 sts).

Next row: Purl.

Next row: K2tog across row (4 sts). Cast off.

Inner ears
make 2

Using 4mm needles and B, cast on 10 sts.

Next row: Purl.

Next row: Inc in each st across row (20 sts).

Work 5 rows st st.

Next row: K2tog across row (10 sts).

Next row: Purl.

Next row: K2tog across row (5 sts).

Next row: Purl. Cast off.

To make up

Sewing up with this type of yarn needs care. Use a big-eyed, blunt-ended needle and short lengths of yarn. Seams will run down the back of the head and body, and the undersides of the arms and legs.

Sew the body seam first, leaving the cast-on end open to stuff. Stuff firmly to give a nice rounded shape. Close the gap. Sew the head in the same way, leaving an opening to stuff. Partially stuff the head as you need to insert safety eyes before closing.

Sew the muzzle seam, which will run underneath. Pin the muzzle to the front of the bear's head and add stuffing to give shape. Now sew it onto the face, adding more stuffing to give a good shape. Sew the nose in place. Insert the eyes on either side of the nose, and click into place. Complete stuffing the head and close the gap.

Stitch the inner and outer ears together. Take some matching yarn, curl the ears into a semi-circular shape, then stitch in place onto the head.

Sew the seams on the arms, and as before, leave the cast-on edge open to enable stuffing. To stuff the arms, push plenty of stuffing down into the paw first then continue stuffing the rest of the arm. Sew the leg seams and stuff as for arms.

Now assemble the bear. Pin on the legs first, noting she is in the sitting position, and get them level if you can. Sew in place. Pin the arms in position as you did with the legs and sew firmly in place. Finally, sew the bear's head onto the body.

Pyjamas

Back of top

Using 4mm needles and C, cast on 38 sts.

Work in k2, p2 rib for 4 rows.

Change to st st and work 32 rows.

Change to k2, p2 rib and work 4 rows.

Cast off.

Front of top

Work as for back until you have completed 8 rows st st.

Work panda's face from chart, reading rows from right to left on RS rows and from left to right on WS rows. You will need to join in separate small balls of C on each side of D, twisting the yarns together on the wrong sides as you do to avoid holes in your work.

Row 1: K17C , k4D, k17C.

Continue until you have worked all 12 rows. Break D and continue in C only.

Complete to match back. Cast off.

Sleeves

make 2

Using 4mm needles and C, cast on 28 sts.

Work 4 rows in k2, p2 rib.

Join in E and D and work in st st in a stripe sequence of 2 rows D, 2 rows E, 2 rows C.

Work 18 rows in st st stripe patt.

Cast off.

PANDA HEAD CHART (12 sts x 12 rows)

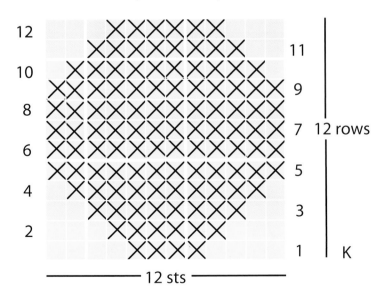

To make up

Sew shoulder seams on back and front for approximately ¾in (2cm). Now sew the sleeves to back and front on either side. Sew the side and sleeve seams.

To make panda features

Using 4mm needles and some black fashion fur yarn, cast on 4 sts. Knit two rows and cast off. Make another piece the same. Sew ears to either side of the head. Using fashion fur, embroider the eyes. Embroider the nose and mouth with black embroidery floss. Sew ribbon to top of head.

Trousers

make 2

Using 4mm needles and C, cast on 40 sts.

Work in k2, p2 rib for 4 rows.

Next row (make holes for cord):
*K2, yrn, p2tog; rep from * to end.

Work 3 more rows in k2, p2 rib.

Join in E and D and work in st st in a stripe sequence of 2 rows D, 2 rows E, 2 rows C.

Work 16 rows st st.

Keeping continuity of stripe sequence throughout, proceed as follows:

Next row: K19, m1, k2, m1, k19 (42 sts).

Next row: Purl.

Next row: K20, m1, k2, m1, k20 (44 sts).

Next row: Purl.

Divide for legs

Next row: K21, cast off 2 sts, k21.

Proceed on first set as follows:

Next row: Purl.

Cont on this set of sts and work in st st stripe sequence until you have completed 34 rows in total decreasing 1 st in the centre of the last row.

Break D and E and cont in C only.

Change to k2, p2 rib and work 4 rows. Cast off in rib.

Work other side to match.

To make up

Sew the side seams and leg seams. Using C, make a twisted cord and thread through waist.

Bow

Using 4mm needles and C, cast on 30 sts.

Work 2 rows in garter stitch.

Join D and work 2 rows garter stitch.

Join E and work 2 rows garter stitch.

Join C and work 2 rows garter stitch.

Cast off.

To make up

Join the short ends. Fold the work in half with the join at centre back. Run a gathering thread of C through the centre of the piece. Draw up firmly to form bow shape. Stitch to bear's head.

Slippers

make 2

Using 4mm needles and E, cast on 30 sts.

Next row: Knit.

Next row: Inc in first and last st (32 sts).

Next row: Knit.

Next row: Inc in first and last st (34 sts).

Knit 2 rows.

Next row: K12, inc in each of next 10 sts, k12 (44 sts).

Knit 10 rows.

Next row: K12, (k2tog) 10 times, k12 (34 sts).

Knit 2 rows. Join in C.

Knit 1 row in C, and cast off.

To make up

Join sole and back seam. Make a tiny pompom (see page 79) and sew to the front of the slipper.

Hot-water bottle
Front

Using 4mm needles and E, cast on 16 sts.

Knit 2 rows.

Inc at each end of next and following alt rows to 20 sts.

Next row: Knit.

Next row: K7, p6, k7.

Repeat last 2 rows 11 times more.

Now dec 1 st at each end of next and following alt rows to 10 sts.

Knit 2 rows.

Now inc 1 st at each end of every row to 16 sts.

Knit 4 rows and cast off.

Back

Work as for front but omit st st panel and just work the piece in garter stitch.

To make up

Sew the back and front together. Leave the top open and stuff lightly. Now stitch along the narrow piece at the top of the bottle, leaving the neck open. Sew or glue a ribbon in place at the base of the neck.

Daisy
& Honey

Knit this super cute mother and child duo to bring a smile to any little child's face. Daisy has a beautiful lacy dress with ribbon ties and Honey has her own tiny romper suit complete with teddy motif.

YOU WILL NEED

For Daisy and Honey

Sirdar Country Style DK, 40% nylon, 30% wool, 30% acrylic (170yds/155m per 50g ball):
3 x 50g balls in 409 Naturelle (A)
Oddment of dark brown yarn for features

Needles size 4mm (UK8:US6)
Safety stuffing

For the dress and romper suit

Sirdar Snuggly DK, 55% nylon, 45% acrylic (179yds/165m per 50g ball):
2 x 50g balls in 252 Lemon (B)
1 x 50g ball in 303 Cream (C)
Oddment in 403 Wobble (D)

Needles size 4mm (UK8: US6)
2yds (2m) narrow double-sided satin baby ribbon
Bear applique motif for romper
Flower and leaf motif for dress

KNITTING NOTES

Tension

22 sts x 28 rows to 4in (10cm) using 4mm (UK8:US6) needles.

Yarn notes

Any DK weight yarn knitting up to a similar tension will work for the bears.

Measurements

Daisy is 11½ in (29cm) tall when sitting. Honey is 6in (15cm) tall when sitting. Circumference of Daisy's tummy when stuffed is about 13½in (34.5cm); Honey's tummy is 7½in (19cm).

Abbreviations

Refer to page 33.

Tip The lacy pattern is a little complicated to follow, so is best not attempted if you are a novice knitter. However, you could knit the skirt of the dress in just stocking stitch if preferred.

Daisy
Body and head
made all in one piece

Using 4mm needles and A, cast on 20 sts.

Next row: Purl.

Next row: Inc in each st across row (40 sts).

Next row: Purl.

Next row: *K1, inc in next st; rep from * to end (60 sts).

Cont in st st without further increases until you have worked 38 more rows (mark this row for neck of bear).

Cont in st st for a further 24 rows.

Shape top of head

Next row: *K4, skpo; rep from * to last st, k1 (50 sts).

Next and following alt rows: Purl.

Next row: *K3, skpo; rep from * to last st, k1 (40 sts).

Next row: *K2, skpo; rep from * to last st, k1 (30 sts).

Next row: *K1, skpo; rep from * to last st, k1 (20 sts).

Next row: Skpo; rep to last st, k1 (10 sts).

Purl 1 row and cast off.

Muzzle

Using 4mm needles and A, cast on 10 sts.

Next row: Purl.

Next row: Inc in each st across row (20 sts).

Next row: Purl.

Next row: *K1, inc in next st; rep from * to end (30 sts).

Next row: Purl.

Next row: *K2, inc in next st; rep from * to end (40 sts).

Next row: Purl.

Next row: *K3, inc in next st; rep from * to end (50 sts).

Next row: Purl.

Next row: *K4, inc in next st; rep from * to end (60 sts).

Next row: Purl.

Work 4 rows st st and cast off.

Ears
make 4
Using 4mm needles and A, cast on 10 sts.

Next row: Purl.

Next row: Inc in each st across row (20 sts).

Beg with a purl row, work 9 rows st st.

Next row: K2tog across row (10 sts).

Next row: Purl.

Next row: K2tog across row and cast off.

Arms
make 2
Using 4mm needles and A, cast on 10 sts.

Next row: Purl.

Next row: *K1, inc in next st; rep from * across row (15 sts).

Next row: Purl.

Next row: *K1, inc in next st; rep from * to last st, k1 (22 sts).

Next row: Purl.

Next row: Inc in first and last st (24 sts).

Beg with a purl row, work 22 rows in st st.

Next row: *K1, skpo; rep from * to end (16 sts).

Next row: Purl.

Next row: K2tog across row (8 sts).

Next row: Purl.

Next row: K2tog across row (4 sts). Break yarn and run through sts left on needle. Draw up and fasten off.

Legs
make 2

Using 4mm needles and A, cast on 10 sts.

Next row: Purl.

Next row: *K1, inc in next st; rep from * across row (15 sts).

Next row: Purl.

Next row: *K1, inc in next st; rep from * to last st, k1 (22 sts).

Next row: Purl.

Next row: Inc in first and last st (24 sts).

Next row: Purl.

Repeat last 2 rows once more (26 sts).

Cont in st st for 24 rows.

Increase for foot

Next row: K9, inc in each of next 8 sts, k9 (34 sts).

Beg with a purl row, work 9 rows st st.

Next row: K2tog across row (17 sts).

Next row: Purl.

Next row: K2tog across row to last st, k1 (9 sts).

Next row: Purl.

Break yarn and run through sts left on needle. Draw up and fasten off.

Nose

Using 4mm needles and dark brown DK yarn, cast on 8 sts.

Work 4 rows st st.

Next row: K2tog, work to last 2 sts, k2tog (6 sts).

Next row: Purl.

Next row: K2tog, k2, k2tog (4 sts).

Next row: Purl.

Next row: K2tog twice (2 sts).

Next row: Purl.

Next row: K2tog and fasten off.

Leave a long tail of yarn as you will use this to form the mouth.

Honey
Body and head
made all in one piece

Using 4mm needles and A, cast on
10 sts.

Next row: Purl.

Next row: Inc in each st across
row (20 sts).

Next row: Purl.

Next row: *K1, inc in next st; rep
from * to end (30 sts).

Next row: Purl.

Work 28 rows in st st (mark this row
as neckline)

Cont in st st for a further 14 rows.

Shape top of head

Next row: *K1, k2tog; rep from *
to end (20 sts).

Next row: Purl.

Next row: K2tog across row
(10 sts).

Next row: Purl.

Next row: K2tog across row (5 sts).
Break yarn and run through sts left
on needle. Draw up and fasten off.

Arms
make 2

Using 4mm needles and A, cast on
7 sts.

Next row: Purl.

Next row: Inc in each st across
row (14 sts).

Next row: Purl.

Work 18 rows in st st.

Next row: K2tog across row (7 sts).

Next row: Purl.

Next row: K2tog 3 times, k1.
Break yarn and run through sts left
on needle. Draw up and fasten off.

Legs
make 2

Using 4mm needles and A, cast on 7 sts.

Next row: Purl.

Next row: Inc in each st across row (14 sts).

Next row: Purl.

Work 16 rows in st st.

Shape foot

Next row: K4, inc in each of next 6 sts, k4 (20 sts).

Next row: Purl.

Work 4 rows in st st.

Next row: K2tog across row (10 sts).

Next row: Purl.

Repeat last 2 rows once more (5 sts).

Next row: K2tog twice, k1.

Break yarn and run through sts left on needle. Draw up and fasten off.

Muzzle

Using 4mm needles and A, cast on 6 sts.

Next row: Purl.

Next row: Inc in each st across row (12 sts).

Next row: Purl.

Next row: *K1, inc in next st; rep from * to end (18 sts).

Next row: Purl.

Next row: *K2, inc in next st; rep from * to end (24 sts).

Next row: Purl.

Work 2 rows st st and cast off.

Ears
make 2

Using 4mm needles and A, cast on 7 sts.

Work 6 rows in st st.

Next row: K2tog, knit to last 2 sts, k2tog (5 sts).

Next row: P2tog, p1, p2tog (3 sts).

Next row: Inc in next st, k1, inc in last st (5 sts).

Next row: Inc in next st, p3, inc in last st (7 sts).

Work 6 rows in st st and cast off.

To make up

For Daisy, begin with the head and body. Sew the seam that runs down the back of the bear, but leave the base open to stuff. Stuff the head first, making it nice and firm and round. Thread a needle with matching yarn and, beginning at the marked row for the neck, weave the yarn in and out of each stitch all the way around, starting and ending at the seam. Pull up quite firmly to form the head

and neck. Secure well at the seam. Continue to stuff the body, then close the base.

Sew the muzzle's side seam to form a cup shape and add some stuffing, then pin to the front of the head. Sew it in place. Pin the nose in the centre of the muzzle with the widest part at the top, add a tiny bit of stuffing to pad it out slightly, then sew in place. Use the long tail of yarn left to stitch it to the base of the muzzle, pulling it firmly to form the bear's mouth.

Embroider the eyes using black yarn. Sew the ears together in pairs and attach to either side of the head.

Sew the arm seams, leaving the top open for stuffing. Attach the arms to the bear's shoulders on either side.

Sew the leg seams and stuff, making sure that you fill out the feet to give a nice shape. Sew the legs to each side of the bear in a sitting position. Stitch the bow (instructions on page 131) to the top of the head.

Sew Honey together in the same way apart from the following differences: her ears are folded over with the right sides inside and the side seams sewn. Turn right sides out, curl the ears and sew onto the head. Embroider a small nose onto the muzzle.

Dress for Daisy
Front

Using 4mm needles and B, cast on 77 sts.

Work 3 rows in garter st.

Row 1 (RS): K1, *yfwd, sl1, k2tog, psso, yfwd, k5; repeat from * to last 4 sts, yfwd, sl1, k2tog, psso, yfwd, k1.

Row 2 (and every following alt row): Purl.

Row 3: As row 1.

Row 5: K4, *yfwd, sl1, k1, psso, k1, k2tog, yfwd, k3; repeat from * to last st, k1.

Row 7: K1, *yfwd, sl1, k2tog, psso, yfwd, k1; repeat from * to end.

Row 8: Purl.

These 8 rows form the pattern and are repeated throughout.

Work another 3 repeats of pattern.

Next row: (K2tog) 15 times, (k3tog) 5 times, (k2tog) 16 times (36 sts).

Next row: Knit.

Next row (make eyelet holes for ribbon): K1, *yfwd, k2tog; rep from * to last st, k1.

Next row: Knit.

Beg with a knit row, work 6 rows st st.

Shape armholes

Cast off 3 sts at beg of next 2 rows (30 sts).

Next row: K1, skpo, knit to last 3 sts, k2tog, k1 (28 sts).

Next row: K1, purl to last st, k1. ***
Repeat last 2 rows until 20 sts remain, ending with a purl row.

Shape neck

Next row: K1, skpo, k4, turn.
Leave rem sts on a stitch holder
or spare needle.

Next row: P2tog, purl to last st, k1
(5 sts).

Next row: K1, skpo, k2 (4 sts).

Next row: P2tog, purl to end
(3 sts).

Next row: Skpo, k1 (2 sts).

Next row: P2tog. Fasten off.
Return to stitches on holder.
Slip centre 6 sts onto holder for
centre neck, rejoin yarn to rem sts
and complete to match other side,
working k2tog instead of skpo.

Back

Work as front to ***

Next row: K1, skpo, k11, turn.
Proceed on this set of sts, leaving
rem sts on a holder.

Next row: K2, purl to last st, k1.

Next row: K1, skpo, knit to end.

Next row: K2, purl to last st, k1.
Cont as on last 2 rows until you
have 6 sts left. Leave on a
stitch holder.
Rejoin yarn to remaining sts and
complete to match first side,
reversing shapings and working
k2tog instead of skpo.

Sleeves

make 2

Using 4mm needles and B, cast on
32 sts.
Work 3 rows in garter st.
Change to st st and work
8 rows.

Shape armholes

Cast off 3 sts at beg of next 2
rows (26 sts).

Next row: Knit.

Next row: K1, purl to last st, k1.
Repeat last 2 rows once more.

Next row: K1, skpo, knit to last 3
sts, k2tog, k1 (24 sts).

Next row: K1, purl to last st, k1.
Repeat last 2 rows until you have
10 sts.
Cast off.

To make up and neckband

Sew raglan seams on back, front
and sleeves. With right side of work
facing and using 4mm needles and
B, beginning at left back, pick up
and knit 6 sts from left back, 10 sts
from first sleeve, 5 sts down side
of neck, 6 sts from front neck, 5 sts
from other side of neck, 10 sts from
sleeve and finally 6 sts from right
back (48 sts).

Next row: Knit.

**Next row (make eyelet holes for
ribbon):** K1, *yfwd, k2tog; rep from
* to last st, k1.

Next row: Knit.

Next row: Cast off.
Join side and sleeve seams. Thread
ribbon through holes at neck and
through holes at waist. Attach
flowers and leaves to front of dress
if desired using fabric glue and
small stitches.

Bow

Using 4mm needles and B, cast on 8 sts.

Knit 58 rows in garter stitch.

Cast off.

To make up

Join the short ends. With the join at centre back, fold the piece in half. Thread a needle with matching yarn and run a gathering thread through the centre of the piece. Draw up firmly to shape the bow.

Romper for Honey

make 2

Using 4mm needles and C, cast on 6 sts.

Knit 2 rows.

Next row: Inc 1 st at each end of row (8 sts).

Next row: Purl.

Repeat last 2 rows twice more (12 sts).

Cast on 2 sts at beg of the next 6 rows (24 sts).

Work 8 rows in st st.

Join in D.

Cont in st st stripe patt as follows:

Work 2 rows D, 2 rows C, 2 rows D, 2 rows C, 2 rows D. Break D.

Cont in C only.

Work 6 rows st st.

Change to k1, p1 rib and work 6 rows. Cast off in rib.

To make up

Sew in the yarn ends. With right sides together, sew the leg seams.

Now sew the side seams, matching the stripes up to the last green stripe. Overlap rib on either side for about ½in (1.5cm) to form the envelope neck. Catch in place with a few stitches.

Attach the baby bear motif to front of the romper if desired using fabric glue and small stitches.

Cute Cubs

These little bears are soft and cuddly and could be the perfect gift for a new baby. The tiny sweater with a heart motif is knitted in a simple T-shape and the motif is added to the front of the sweater using the intarsia method for a special touch.

YOU WILL NEED

For each Cute Cub
Wendy Peter Pan DK, 60% acrylic, 40% nylon (186yds/170m per 50g ball):
2 x 50g balls in 919 Tulip (A) or in 926 Powder Blue (B)
Oddment of dark grey yarn for features

Needles size 4mm (UK8:US6)
Needles size 3.25mm (UK10:US3)
Safety stuffing

For the sweaters
Wendy Peter Pan DK:
1 x 50g ball in 330 Soft Cream (C)

Needles size 4mm (UK8:US6)

USEFUL INFORMATION

Tension
24sts x 32 rows to 4in (10cm) using 4mm (UK8:US6) needles.

Yarn notes
Any DK weight yarn can be substituted as long as it works up to a similar tension. This bear is worked entirely in garter stitch.

Measurements
8in (20cm) tall when sitting. Circumference of tummy when stuffed is about 11¾in (30cm).

Abbreviations
Refer to page 33.

Tip For those who don't feel confident with intarsia, then the motif can be embroidered onto the knitted fabric using the Swiss-darning method (see page 27) or the sweaters can be left plain.

Cute Cub

worked entirely in garter stitch

Head

Using 4mm needles and either A or B, cast on 42 sts.

Knit 4 rows.

Next row: K2tog at each end of row (40 sts).

Knit 2 rows.

Repeat the last 3 rows until 4 sts remain.

Next row: K2tog twice (2 sts).

Next row: K2tog and fasten off.

Muzzle

Using either A or B and 4mm needles, cast on 12 sts.

Next row: Knit.

Next row: Inc 1 st each end of row (14 sts).

Repeat last row once more (16 sts).

Next row: Cast on 2 sts at beg of the next 2 rows (20 sts).

Knit 6 rows.

Next row: Cast off 2 sts at beg of the next 2 rows (16 sts).

Next row: K2tog at each end of row (14 sts).

Repeat last row once more (12 sts).

Knit 2 rows.

Cast off.

Arms

make 2

Using 4mm needles and either A or B, cast on 8 sts.

Knit 1 row.

Next row: Inc in each stitch across row (16 sts).

Knit 2 rows.

Next row: Inc 1 st at each end of next and following alt rows until you have 22 sts.

Knit 20 rows.

Decrease for top of arm

Next row: K2tog at each end of row (20 sts).

Next row: Knit.

Next row: K2tog across row (10 sts).

Cast off. This is the top of the arm.

Body

make 2

Using either A or B and 4mm needles, cast on 16 sts.

Knit 4 rows.

Inc 1 st each end of next and following alt rows until you have 26 sts.

Knit 36 rows.

Dec 1 st each end of next and following alt rows until 14 sts remain.

Cast off. This is the neck edge.

Legs
make 2
Using either A or B and 4mm
needles, cast on 16 sts.
Knit 1 row.
Next row: Inc in each st across
row (32 sts).
Knit 12 rows.
Next row: K10, k2tog 6 times, k10
(26 sts).
Knit 26 rows.
Next row: K2tog at each end of row
(24 sts).
Next row: Knit.
Next row: K2tog across row
(12 sts).
Cast off.

Ears
make 2
Using either A or B and 4mm
needles, cast on 8 sts.
Knit 1 row.
Inc 1 st at each end of next 5 rows
(18 sts).
Knit 4 rows.
Next row: K2tog across row (9 sts).
Next row: K2tog 4 times, k1 (5 sts).
Cast off.

To make up

Take the head triangle and sew together as shown in diagram. Stuff the head quite firmly, shaping as you go. Pin the muzzle to the front of the head, placing it centrally. Add some stuffing to pad it out and then sew it in place, using the photos as a guide.

Embroider the eyes and nose with grey yarn. After working the nose, take the yarn centrally through the nose and pull down to make a line for the mouth, pulling the yarn quite tight to get the shape of the muzzle.

Sew an ear to each corner of the head. Sew the back and front body together, leaving the neck open, and stuff firmly to give a nice shape. Sew the base of the head to the body. Sew the arm and leg seams, with the seams running underneath the pieces.

Stuff each piece quite firmly. Sew an arm to either side of body at shoulder level. Sew the legs in place on either side of the body, in a sitting position.

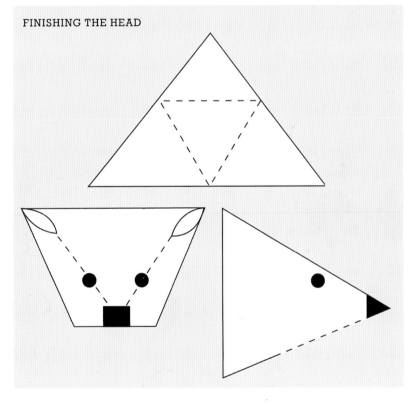

FINISHING THE HEAD

Sweater
Back

Using 4mm needles and C, cast on 33 sts.

Row 1: *K1, p1; rep from * to last st, k1.

Repeat last row 4 times more.

Change to st st and work 26 rows.

Next row: *K1, p1; rep from * to last st, k1.

Repeat last row 5 times more.

Cast off.

Front

Using 4mm needles and C, cast on 33 sts.

Row 1: *K1, p1; rep from * to last st, k1.

Repeat last row 4 times more.

Change to st st and work 8 rows.

Begin to work heart motif

You will need to use 2 separate balls of C on either side of motif, twisting yarns together when changing colours to avoid holes in your work.

Work 13 rows from chart A, reading RS rows from right to left and WS rows from left to right. The chart is worked on the centre 13 stitches. First row will read as follows:

Row 1: K16 C, k1 (A or B), k16 C.

After completing these rows, cont in st st and using only C, beg with a purl row work a further 5 rows.

Next row: *K1, p1; rep from * to last st, k1.

Repeat last row 5 times more and cast off in pattern.

Sleeves
make 2

Using 4mm needles and C, cast on 25 sts.

Next row: *K1, p1; rep from * to last st, k1.

Repeat last row 4 times more.

Change to st st and work 18 rows.

Cast off.

Heart for foot

Using 3.25mm needles and C, cast on 3 sts.

Next row: Purl.

Next row: Inc in each of next 2 sts, k1 (5 sts).

Next row: Purl.

Next row: Inc 1 at each end of row (7 sts).

Next row: Purl.

Repeat last 2 rows until you have 13 sts on the needle, ending with a purl row.

Work 2 rows in st st.

Next row: K2tog at each end of row (11 sts).

Divide for heart shape

Next row: P2tog, p3, place these 4 sts on hold; bind of 1 st (1 st remains on rh needle) p2, p2tog.

Next row: K2tog twice.

Next row: Purl.

Next row: K2tog and fasten off. Return to remaining 4 sts and complete to match first side.

To make up

Sew the shoulder seams overlapping the top at each side to form an envelope neck. Sew the sleeves to either side of back and fronts. Fold the sweater in half and sew the sleeve and side seams. Slip onto the bear over his legs, as it is easier to put the sweater on this way. Take the small heart made for the foot and swiss embroider a small heart in the middle of it, working from chart B.

CHART A (11 sts x 13 rows)

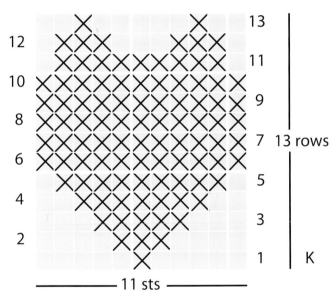

CHART B (7 sts x 6 rows)

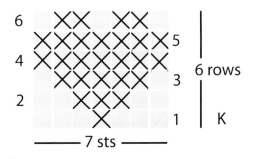

Bella

This sweet grey bear will be the perfect gift for any budding ballet dancer. With her pretty pink top and netted skirt, ribbon-tied ballet shoes and headband with a bow, she's all ready to be star of the show.

YOU WILL NEED

For Bella

Jarol Heritage DK, 55% wool, 25% acrylic, 20% nylon (270yds/250m per 100g ball):
2 x 100g balls in 138 Charcoal (A)
Oddment of black DK yarn features

Needles size 4mm (UK8:US6)
Safety stuffing

For the ballet outfit

DMC Woolly DK, 100% wool (136yds/125m per 50g ball):
3 x 50g balls in 043 Deep Pink (B)

Needles size 4mm (UK8:US6)
3¼yds (3m) of narrow satin double-sided ribbon to match
A small piece of white net fabric approximately 16 x 8in (40 x 20cm)
Fine shirring elastic
Embroidery thread in wine and medium green

KNITTING NOTES

Tension

22 sts x 28 rows to 4in (10cm) using 4mm (UK8:US6) needles.

Yarn notes

Any DK weight yarn will work with this project. Check your tension beforehand and change needle size if needed.

Measurements

10in (26cm) tall when sitting. Circumference of tummy when stuffed is about 13½in (34.5cm).

Abbreviations

Refer to page 33.

Bella

Head

Next row: Using 4mm needles and A, cast on 8 sts.

Next row: Purl.

Next row: Inc in each st across row (16 sts).

Next row: Purl.

Next row: K4, m1, k8, m1, k4 (18 sts).

Next row: Purl.

Next row: K4, m1, k1, m1, k8, m1, k1, m1, k4 (22 sts).

Next row: Purl.

Next row: K5, m1, k1, m1, k10, m1, k1, m1, k5 (26 sts).

Cont increasing like this until you have 66 sts, ending on a purl row. Work 10 rows st st decreasing 1 stitch at either end of row on the final row (64 sts).

Decrease for back of head

Next row: * K6, k2tog; rep from * to end (56 sts).

Next and following alt rows: Purl.

Next row: * K5, k2tog; rep from * to end (48 sts).

Next row: * K4, k2tog; rep from * to end (40 sts).

Next row: * K3, k2tog; rep from * to end (32 sts).

Next row: * K2, k2tog; rep from * to end (24 sts).

Next row: * K1, k2tog; rep from * to end (16 sts).

Next row: K2tog across row (8 sts). Break yarn and run through sts left on needle. Draw up and fasten off.

Body

Using 4mm needles and A, cast on 20 sts.

Next row: Purl.

Next row: Inc in each st across row (40 sts).

Next row: Purl.

Next row: *K1, inc in next st; rep from * to end (60 sts).

Cont in st st for a further 46 rows.

Decrease for top of body

Next row: *K4, k2tog; rep from * to end (50 sts).

Next and following alt rows: Purl.

Next row: *K3, k2tog; rep from * to end (40 sts).

Next row: *K2, k2tog; rep from * to end (30 sts).

Next row: *K1, k2tog; rep from * to end (20 sts).

Next row: K2tog across row (10 sts).

Break yarn and run through sts left on needle. Draw up and fasten off.

Ears

make 4

Using 4mm needles and A, cast on 10 sts.

Work 2 rows st st.

Inc in first and last st on every alt row to 16 sts.

Beg with a purl row, work 7 rows st st.

Next row: K2tog across row (8 sts).

Next row: Purl.

Next row: K2tog across row (4 sts). Cast off.

Arms

make 2

Using 4mm needles and A, cast on 10 sts.

Next row: Purl.

Next row: *K1, inc in next st; rep from * across row (15 sts).

Next row: Purl.

Next row: *K1, inc in next st; rep from * to last st, k1 (22 sts).

Next row: Purl.

Next row: Inc in first and last st (24 sts).

Beg with a purl row, work 27 rows st st.

Next row: *K1, skpo; rep from * to end (16 sts).

Next row: Purl.

Next row: K2tog across row (8 sts).

Next row: Purl.

Next row: K2tog across row (4 sts). Break yarn and run through sts left on needle. Draw up and fasten off.

Legs

make 2

Using 4mm needles and A, cast on 10 sts.

Next row: Purl.

Next row: *K1, inc in next st; rep from * across row (15 sts).

Next row: Purl.

Next row: *K1, inc in next st; rep from * to last st, k1 (22 sts).

Next row: Purl.

Next row: Inc in first and last st (24 sts).

Next row: Purl.

Repeat last 2 rows once more (26 sts).

Cont in st st for 24 rows.

Increase for foot

Next row: K9, inc in each of next 8 sts, k9 (34 sts).

Next row: Purl.

Next row: K12, inc in each of next 10 sts, k12 (44 sts).

Beg with a purl row, work 9 rows st st.

Next row: K2tog across row (22 sts).

Next row: Purl.

Next row: K2tog across row (11 sts).

Next row: Purl.

Next row: K2tog across row to last st, k1 (6 sts).

Break yarn and run through sts left on needle. Draw up and fasten off.

Use the tail of yarn left on the nose to make the line for the mouth. Using some black yarn, embroider the eyes onto the face, and tug them a little to create indentations and add shape to the nose. Attach the head to the body. Sew the seams on the arms and legs, all seams run on the underside of the pieces. Stuff the limbs fairly firmly and pin in position. Sew the limbs in place.

Ballet top
Back
Using 4mm needles and B, cast on 40 sts.
Knit 3 rows.
Work 2 rows st st.
Next row (eyelet holes): K1, *yfwd, k2tog, k2; rep from * ending last rep, k1.
Next row: Purl.
Work 6 rows st st.

Nose
Using 4mm needles and black yarn, cast on 8 sts.
Work 4 rows in st st.
Next row: K2tog, work to last 2 sts, K2tog (6 sts).
Next row: Purl.
Next row: K2tog, k2, k2tog (4 sts).
Next row: Purl.
Next row: K2tog twice.
Next row: Purl.
Next row: K2tog and fasten off.
Leave a long tail of yarn as you will use this to form the mouth.

To make up
Sew the body seam, which runs down the back, and stuff firmly before closing. Sew the head seam and stuff firmly, as with the body. Sew the ears together in pairs, curling them inwards as you do. Sew the ears to either side of the head. Pin the nose in place on the head and pad it out with a little stuffing before stitching it in place.

Begin armhole shaping

Cast off 4 sts at the beg of the next 2 rows (32 sts).

Next row: K2, skpo, knit to last 4 sts, k2tog, k2 (30 sts).

Next row: K2, purl to last 2 sts, k2.

Cont to decrease as on last 2 rows until you have 12 sts.

Cast off.

Sleeves
make 2

Follow instructions as for back but work 4 rows st st instead of 6.

Left front

Using 4mm needles and B, cast on 40 sts.

Knit 3 rows.

Next row: Knit.

Next row: K2, purl to end.

Next row (eyelet holes): K1, *yfwd, k2tog, k2;

rep from * ending last rep, yfwd, k2tog, k5.

Next row: K2, purl to end.

Next row: Knit to last 4 sts, k2tog, k2 (39 sts).

Next row: K2, purl to end.

Repeat last 2 rows twice more.

Begin armhole shaping

Cast off 4sts, knit to last 4 sts, k2tog, k2 (32 sts).

Next row: K2, purl to last 2 sts, k2.

Next row: K2, skpo, knit to last 4 sts, k2tog, k2 (30 sts).

Next row: K2, p2tog, purl to last 2 sts, k2 (29 sts).

Next row: Dec at armhole edge on every alt row and at the same time dec on front edge on every row until you have 5 sts.

Knit 4 rows garter stitch and cast off.

Right front

Using 4mm needles and B, cast on 40 sts.

Knit 3 rows.

Next row: Knit.

Next row: Purl to last 2 sts, k2.

Next row (eyelet holes): K5, *yfwd, k2tog, k2; rep from * ending last rep, yfwd, k2tog, k1.

Next row: Purl to last 2 sts, k2.

Next row: K2, skpo, knit to end (39 sts).

Next row: Purl to last 2 sts, k2.

Repeat last 2 rows twice more.

Next row: K2, skpo, knit to end (36 sts).

Begin armhole shaping

Next row: Cast off 4 sts, purl to last 2 sts, k2 (32 sts).

Next row: K2, skpo, knit to end (31 sts).

Next row: K2, p2tog, purl to last 4 sts, p2tog tbl, k2 (29 sts).

Next row: K2, skpo, knit to end (28 sts).

Next row: Dec at armhole edge on every alt row and at the same time dec at front edge on every row to 5 sts.
Knit 4 rows garter stitch and cast off.

To make up

Join the sleeve seams neatly to the back and fronts. Join the sleeve and side seams. Cut the ribbon into lengths and thread through the holes at the base of the top. Sew two shorter pieces of ribbon at each side seam to enable you to tie the top. Thread ribbon through the sleeves and neatly sew the ends together on the inside of the sleeve. Using the wine and green embroidery thread, embroider flowers and leaves onto one side of the top if desired.

Skirt

make 2

Using 4mm needles and B, cast on 42 sts.
Knit 2 rows.
Next row: K13, m1, p1, m1, k14, m1, p1, m1, k13 (46 sts).
Next row: P13, k3, p14, k3, p13.
Next row: K13, m1, p3, m1, k14, m1, p3, m1, k13 (50 sts).
Next row: P13, k5, p14, k5, p13.
Next row: K13, m1, p5, m1, k14, m1, p5, m1, k13 (54 sts).
Next row: P13, k7, p14, k7, p13.
Continue to increase in this way, adding 1 st each side of the panels on every alt row until you have 15 sts in each panel.

Next row: K13, p15, k14, p15, k13.
Next row: P13, k15, p14, k15, p13.
Repeat last 2 rows 3 times more. Work 4 rows garter stitch and cast off.

To make up

Before sewing the seam of the skirt you need to measure its length and depth. Now using the skirt as a template, cut a piece of net twice as long and twice as deep as the skirt. Fold the net in half lengthways, the folded end is to be at the bottom of the skirt. Pin the top edge closed.

Take a needle threaded with some shirring elastic and sew a neat running stitch all along the edge, sewing through both thicknesses of net. Gather up to fit the waist of the skirt. Stitch neatly to the inside of waist of the skirt.Sew the back seam neatly. Join the side seams.

Thread fine shirring elastic through the top of the skirt, weaving in and out of the fabric. Tie the elastic in a tight knot, and work in the ends.

Headband

Using 4mm needles and B, cast on
76 sts.
Knit 4 rows and cast off.

Bow

Using 4mm needles and B, cast on
7 sts.
Knit 60 rows.
Cast off.

To make up

Sew the short ends of the headband
together, then sew the short ends
of the bow together. Fold in half
with the seam at the centre back.

Run a gathering thread through
the centre of the piece and draw
up to form a bow shape. Sew the
bow to the centre of the headband.
Embroider flowers and leaves into
the centre of the bow if desired.

Shoes

make 2

Using 4mm needles and B, cast on
8 sts.
Next row: Purl.
Next row: Inc in each st across
row (16 sts).
Next row: Purl.
Next row: *K1, inc in next st; rep
from * to end (24 sts).
Next row: Purl.
Next row: *K2, inc in next st; rep
from * to end (32 sts).
Next row: Purl.

Next row: *K3, inc in next st; rep
from * to end (40 sts).
Work in st st for 10 rows.
Next row: K1, *yfwd, k2tog, k2;
rep from * ending last rep, k1.
Next row: Purl.
Knit 2 rows and cast off.

To make up

Sew the back seam. Thread ribbon
through the holes at the ankles.

Benji

Everyone will love this fun skater bear with his endearing face and his own special hoodie complete with bear ears! He even has his own skateboard, making him the coolest bear around. He is made in a soft brushed yarn and is just waiting to be hugged.

• •

YOU WILL NEED

For Benji
Sirdar Freya, 55% cotton, 31% acrylic, 14% polyester (120yds/110m per 50g ball): 2 x 50g balls in 857 Gosling (A) Oddment of black DK yarn for nose (B)

Needles size 5.5mm (UK5:US9) Needles size 4mm (UK8:US6) Safety stuffing 1 pair of black button safety eyes

For the hoodie
Sirdar Country Style DK, 40% nylon, 30% wool, 30% acrylic (170yds/155m per 50g ball): 1 x 50g ball in 614 Meadow (C) 1 x 50g ball in 399 Honey (D)

Needles size 4mm (UK8:US6)

For the skateboard
Sirdar Country Style DK: 1 x 50g ball in 399 Honey (F) Robin DK, 100% acrylic (82 yds/75m per 25g ball) 2 x 25g ball 6392 Seal (E) 2 x 25g ball in 162 Cordial (G) Oddment of blue DK yarn

Needles size 4mm (UK8:US6) Stiff card Craft glue

KNITTING NOTES

Tension
15 sts x 20 rows to 4in (10cm) over st st for Freya using 5.5mm (UK5:US9) needles. 22 sts x 28 rows to 4in (10cm) over st st for DK using 4mm (UK8:US6) needles.

Yarn notes
Any aran-type yarn with a tension to match the bear will do if you need to substitute yarns.

Measurements
11in (28cm) tall when sitting. Circumference of tummy when stuffed is about 14in (35.5cm).

Abbreviations
Refer to page 33.

Benji
Head

Using 5.5mm needles and A, cast on 10 sts.

Next row: Purl.

Next row: Inc in each st across row (20 sts).

Beg with a purl row, work 3 rows st st.

Next row: *K1, inc in next st; repeat from * to end (30 sts).

Beg with a purl row, work 3 rows st st.

Next row: *K1, inc in next st; repeat from * to end (45 sts).

Beg with a purl row, work 11 rows st st.

Shape top of head

Next row: *K1, k2tog; rep from * to end of row (30 sts).

Beg with a purl row, work 3 rows st st.

Next row: K2tog across row (15 sts).

Next row: Purl.

Break yarn and run through sts left on needle. Draw up and fasten off.

Muzzle

Using 5.5mm needles and A, cast on 8 sts.

Next row: Purl.

Next row: Inc in each stitch across row (16 sts).

Next row: Purl.

Next row: *K1, inc in next st; rep from * to end (24 sts).

Next row: Purl.

Next row: *K2, inc in next st; rep from * to end (32 sts).

Beg with a purl row, work 7 rows st st.

Cast off.

Nose

Using 4mm needles and B, cast on 8 sts.

Work 6 rows garter st.

Dec 1 st at each end of next and following alt rows to 2 sts.

Next row: K2tog, fasten off, leaving a long tail of yarn.

Body

Using 5.5mm needles and A, cast on 10 sts.

Next row: Purl.

Next row: Inc in each st across row (20 sts).

Beg with a purl row, work 3 rows st st.

Next row: *K1, inc in next st; rep from * to end (30 sts).

Beg with a purl row, work 3 rows st st.

Next row: *K1, inc in next st; rep from * to end (45 sts).

Beg with a purl row, work 31 rows st st.

Shape top of body

Next row: *K1, k2tog; rep from * to end of row (30 sts).

Beg with a purl row, work 3 rows st st.

Next row: K2tog across row (15 sts).

Next row: Purl.

Break yarn and run through sts left on needle. Draw up and fasten off.

Legs
make 2

Using 5.5mm needles and A, cast on 8 sts.

Next row: Purl.

Next row: Inc in each st across row (16 sts).

Work in st st for 5 rows.

Next row: Inc 1 st at each end of row (18 sts).

Work 3 rows st st.

Next row: *K2, inc in next st; rep from * to end (24 sts).

Work 17 rows st st.

Next row: K8, inc in each of next 8 sts, k8 (32 sts).

Next row: Purl.

Work 8 rows st st.

Next row: K2tog across row (16 sts).

Next row: Purl.

Repeat last 2 rows once more. Break yarn and run through sts left on needle. Draw up and fasten off.

Arms
make 2
Using 5.5mm needles and A, cast on 8 sts.

Next row: Purl.

Next row: Inc in each st across row (16 sts).

Next row: Purl.

Next row: Inc 1 st at each end (18 sts).

Next row: Purl.

Next row: Inc 1 st at each end (20 sts).

Next row: Purl.

Work 18 rows st st.

Next row: K2tog across row (10 sts).

Next row: Purl.

Next row: K2tog across row (5 sts).

Next row: Purl.

Break yarn and run through sts left on needle. Draw up and fasten off.

Ears
make 2
Using 5.5mm needles and A, cast on 10 sts.

Next row: Purl.

Next row: Inc in each st across row (20 sts).

Work 5 rows st st.

Next row: K2tog across row (10 sts).

Next row: Purl.

Next row: K2tog across row (5 sts).

Cast off.

To make up
Sewing up with this type of yarn needs care. Use a big-eyed, blunt-ended needle and short lengths of yarn. Seams will run down the back of the head and body, and the undersides of the arms and legs.

Sew the body seam first, leaving the cast-on end open to stuff. Stuff firmly to give a nice rounded shape. Close the gap.

Sew the head and sew in the same way, leaving an opening to stuff. Stuff firmly.

Sew the arm seams, and as before, leave the cast-on edge open to enable stuffing. To stuff the arms, push plenty of stuffing down into the paw first, then continue stuffing the rest of the arm.

Sew the leg seams, leaving the top open to stuff. Stuff firmly, pushing extra stuffing into the feet.

To make up, cont'd

Sew the muzzle seam; this will run underneath. Pin to the front of the bear's head and add stuffing. This will take a bit of time and patience to get it to look good. Now sew it onto the face, adding more stuffing to give a good shape. Sew the nose onto the centre of the muzzle.

Now insert safety eyes on either side of the head just above the muzzle. Click into place, and close the base of the head.

Pin the ears onto the head on either side. Try to get them level. Take some matching yarn, curl the ears into a semi-circular shape, then stitch them in place.

Now assemble the bear. Pin on his legs first, noting he is in the sitting position, get them level if you can. Sew the legs in place. Pin the arms in position as you did with the legs. Sew firmly in place. Finally, sew the bear's head onto the body.

Hoodie
Back

Using 4mm needles and C, cast on 38 sts.

Work in double moss st as follows:

Row 1: *K2, p2; repeat from * to last 2 sts, k2.

Row 2: *P2, k2; repeat from * to last 2 sts, p2.

Row 3: *P2, k2; repeat from * to last 2 sts, p2.

Row 4: *K2, p2; repeat from * to last 2 sts, k2.

Repeat first 2 rows once more.
Change to st st and work 16 rows.

Shape arms

Cast off 2 sts at beg of next 2 rows (34 sts).

Next row: K1, skpo, knit to last 3 sts, k2tog, k1 (32 sts).

Next row: K1, purl to last st, k1.
Repeat last 2 rows to 14 sts, ending with a purl row.
Cast off.

Sleeves
make 2

Using 4mm needles and C, cast on 36 sts.

Work 4 rows in double moss st.
Join in D, change to st st and work in stripes of 2 rows D, 2 rows C, for 14 rows.

Keeping continuity of stripe sequence, shape armholes

Cast off 2 sts at beg of next 2 rows (32 sts).

Work 2 rows in st st.

Next row: K1, skpo, knit to last 3 sts, k2tog, k1 (30 sts).

Next row: K1, purl to last st, k1.
Repeat last 2 rows to 12 sts, ending with a purl row.
Cast off.

Right front

Using 4mm needles and C, cast on 20 sts.

Work in double moss st as follows:

Row 1: *K2, p2; repeat from * to end.

Row 2: *P2, k2; repeat from * to end.

Row 3: *P2, k2; repeat from * to end.

Row 4: *K2, p2; repeat from * to end.

Repeat first 2 rows once more.

Change to st st with double moss st front border.

Next row: P2, k2, p2, knit to end.

Next row: Purl to last 6 sts, k2, p2, k2.

Keeping double moss st border correct, work a further 13 rows. (Work 14 rows for left front.)

Shape armhole

Next row: Cast off 2 sts, pattern to end (18 sts).

Next row: Pattern to last 3 sts, k2tog, k1 (17 sts).

Next row: K1, pattern to end.

Repeat last 2 rows twice more (15 sts).

Shape neck

Next row: Cast off 6 sts, pattern to last 3 sts, k2tog, k1 (8 sts).

Next row: K1, purl to end.

Cont to dec at armhole edge as before until 2 sts remain, k2tog and fasten off.

Left front

Work as for right front but reverse border and shapings.

Hood

Begin at back.

Using 4mm needles and C, cast on 24 sts.

Work in striped pattern as for sleeves for 28 rows.

Keeping pattern sequence correct

Next 2 rows: Cast on 24 sts, work to end (72 sts).

Cont in stripes for another 16 rows.

Work 4 rows double moss st in C only. Cast off.

Ears

make 2

Using 4mm needles and D, cast on 6 sts.

Work 2 rows st st.

Inc 1 st at each end of next and alt rows to 10 sts.

Work 16 rows st st.

Dec 1 st at each end of next and following alt rows to 6 sts.

Work 2 rows st st and cast off.

To make up

Sew the sleeves to back and fronts. Using 4mm needles and C, join yarn to right front neck edge after cast off stitches, pick up and knit 6 sts along neck edge, 12 sts from first sleeve, 14 sts across back, 12 sts from second sleeve and 6 sts down left front neck edge (50 sts).

Next row: *K2, p2; repeat from * to last 2 sts, k2.

Next row: *P2,k; repeat from * to last 2 sts, P2.

Cast off firmly.

Sew in the yarn ends, join the side and sleeve seams. Take the hood and join the short sides to the back to form the hood. Pin the base of the hood all around the neck band, ease if needed. Sew neatly in place. Take the ear and fold in half, join short sides and turn right side out. Sew the base of the ear to corner of hood. Repeat with second ear. Make two twisted cords in D and join to either side of the fronts, tie in a bow.

Skateboard
Back and front
make 1 in E and 1 in F for both back and front, 4 pieces in total

Using 4mm needles and appropriate colour, cast on 14 sts.
Work 2 rows in st st.
Next row: Inc in first and last st (16 sts).
Next row: Purl.
Now cast on 2 sts at the beg of the next 4 rows (24 sts).
Work 14 rows st st.
Next row: K2tog at each end of row (22 sts).
Next row: Purl.
Work 20 rows st st.
Cast off 2 sts at the beg of the next 6 rows (10 sts).
Cast off remaining 10 sts.

Wheels
make 4
Using 4mm needles and G, cast on 10 sts.
Knit 34 rows garter st and cast off.

Axles
make 2
Using 4mm needles and E, cast on 36 sts.
Work 14 rows in st st and cast off.

Wheel inners
make 4
Using 4mm needles and blue yarn, cast on 3 sts.
Next row: Knit.
Next row: K1, inc in next st, k1 (4 sts).
Next row: Knit.
Next row: Knit.
Next row: K1, k2tog, k1 (3 sts).
Next row: K3tog and fasten off.

To make up
Cut a piece of stiff card into an oblong 7½in (19cm) x 4¼in (11cm). Round off the top and bottom, tapering the top third of the board in a little. With right sides facing, sew the two pieces of the board together, leaving the base open. Turn right sides out. Carefully spread a little craft glue all around the top edge of the card. Slip it carefully into the knitted piece, and press down firmly all around the edges. Sew the base neatly closed.

Roll a tube of card into a cylinder measuring 6½in (16cm) long x 2½in (7cm) in circumference. Glue the edges together firmly. Take the axle covering and sew the long edges together to form a tube. Push the card tube inside.

Fold a wheel piece in half lengthwise and join the short ends to form a ring. Do the same with the other three wheels. Slip a wheel onto both ends of the axles and glue them in place. You may also sew in place to make them extra secure. Sew or glue the wheel inners in place inside each wheel. Pin axles to base of skateboard and glue or sew in place.

Suppliers

Below is a list of suppliers' websites and links for the yarns and materials used in this book. Some suppliers will stock all of the yarns required and many ship worldwide. Although specific yarns are listed in each pattern, most yarns can be substituted as long as they have a similar tension.

Bergère de France

For contacts in the UK and Ireland:
www.bergeredefrance.co.uk
For contacts in Europe and worldwide:
www.bergeredefrance.com

Hobbycraft

Hobbycraft stores are located all over the UK. They stock just about everything you will need to create the bears, from yarns and needles, to toy stuffing and fabric glues:
www.hobbycraft.co.uk

Rico Yarns

Rico Design GmbH & Co. KG
Industriestr. 19–23
33034 Brakel
Germany
+49 (0) 52 72 602-0
info@rico-design.de

Sirdar Yarns

Flanshaw Lane
Wakefield
West Yorkshire,
WF2 9ND
UK
+44 (0)1924 231682
www.sirdar.co.uk/storelocator
www.sirdar.co.uk/contactus/
findsirdarworldwide

Wendy Wools Ltd

Thomas B. Ramsden
Gordon Mills
Netherfield Road
Guiseley
West Yorkshire,
LS20 9PD
UK
+44 (0)1943 872 264
www.tbramsden.co.uk

Other yarns used in the book can be bought from many online stockists who will ship worldwide.
www.deramores.com
www.loveknitting.com

About the author

Val's passion for knitting and needlecrafts began when she was a little girl: her father taught her to knit when she was just five years old. As she grew up she became more proficient at knitting and began to work for spinners and designers, checking knitting patterns and making garments for photography. She decided to make her own creations and soon knitting magazines were publishing her work on a regular basis. About five years ago she wrote her first book, which became very popular, and she went on to write many more bestselling knitting and crochet books, which are available worldwide. Val also teaches knitting and crochet, and lives and works in Shropshire in the UK. Her website can be found at www.crossedneedles.co.uk

Acknowledgements

Many thanks to Sirdar, Rico, Bergère de France and Thomas Ramsden for their kind supply of some of the yarns used in the books. A big thank you to Dominique Page and everyone at GMC for their never-ending help, encouragement and wonderful work in producing this gorgeous publication. And last but not least, thank you to all my family and friends who have supported me and offered endless advice and help while I was creating all the bears in the book.

Index

To place an order, or to request a catalogue, contact:

GMC Publications Ltd

Castle Place, 166 High Street, Lewes, East Sussex, BN7 1XU

United Kingdom

Tel: +44 (0)1273 488005

www.gmcbooks.com